simply *more* INDIAN

More Sweet and Spicy Recipes
from India, Pakistan and East Africa

Tahera Rawji

whitecap

Whitecap Books

Whitecap Books is known for its expertise in the cookbook market, and has produced some of the most innovative and familiar titles found in kitchens across North America. Visit our website at www.whitecap.ca.

Edited by Elaine Jones and Taryn Boyd
Proofread by Ann-Marie Metten
Design by Michelle Mayne
Food photography by Tracey Kusiewicz
Pantry and kitchen tools photography by Michelle Mayne
Bowl illustration by Janos Sitar

Printed in Canada by Friesens

Library and Archives Canada Cataloguing in Publication

Rawji, Tahera
Simply more Indian : more sweet and spicy recipes from India, Pakistan and East Africa / Tahera Rawji.

Includes index.
ISBN 978-1-55285-931-5

1. Cookery, Indic. 2. Cookery, Pakistani. 3. Cookery, African.
I. Title.

TX724.5.I4R383 2008   641.5954   C2008-900650-X

The publisher acknowledges the financial support of the Government of Canada through the Book Publishing Industry Development Program (BPIDP) and the Province of British Columbia through the Book Publishing Tax Credit.

08 09 10 11 12   5 4 3 2 1

This book is dedicated to my husband, Shaukat,
my daughter, Safinaaz, and my son, Zuher,
without whose help and support (and taste-testing!)
I would not have been able to create this book

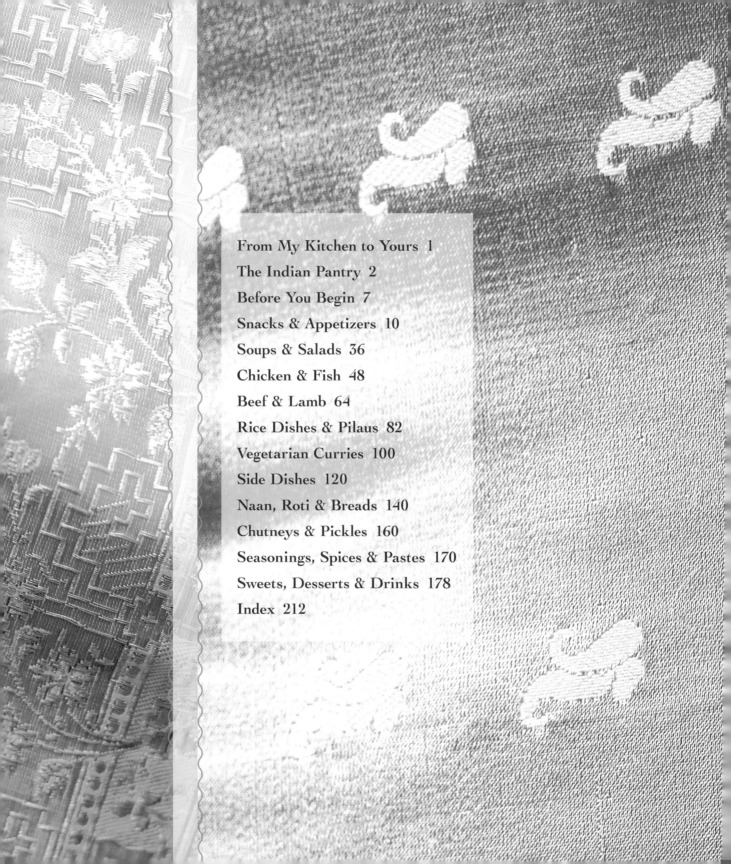

From My Kitchen to Yours 1

The Indian Pantry 2

Before You Begin 7

Snacks & Appetizers 10

Soups & Salads 36

Chicken & Fish 48

Beef & Lamb 64

Rice Dishes & Pilaus 82

Vegetarian Curries 100

Side Dishes 120

Naan, Roti & Breads 140

Chutneys & Pickles 160

Seasonings, Spices & Pastes 170

Sweets, Desserts & Drinks 178

Index 212

Contents

Acknowledgments

I would like to thank Rukhsana Rawji, Sharmina Kermalli, Shabnam Dewji and Nathan Hyam for assisting in preparing food for the photo shoots.

I would like to also thank the following people and establishments for providing dishes and props for the photo shoot: Manek Purbhai, Rukhsana Rawji, Shamim Jagani, Pushpa Sharan, Mumtaz Nathu, Nathan Hyam and Punjab Foods of Main Street, Vancouver.

From My Kitchen to Yours

I was born in Zanzibar off the East African Coast and grew up surrounded by the island's abundant and amazing spices. My passion for cooking led to a career as a cooking instructor.

The idea of recording my recipes came from my cousins. They got tired of calling me from India, the Middle East, and London to ask me how to prepare this and that. Writing down my family's favorite recipes led to *Simply Indian: Sweet and Spicy Recipes from India, Pakistan and East Africa*. I had many more recipes to share, so I wrote *Simply More Indian: More Sweet and Spicy Recipes from India, Pakistan and East Africa*.

Cooking Indian food does not have to be difficult! It largely depends on two factors: the correct use of spices and the correct cooking methods. This book teaches you both. I've included a special pantry section introducing unfamiliar ingredients (see pages 2–5). You'll also find *Tahera's Tips* throughout the book, which offer more information about specific ingredients.

Simply More Indian is designed to help you grasp the flavors integral to Indian cooking. While all the methods are not necessarily traditional, they will enable you to create authentic Indian tastes. I hope my creations will encourage culinary adventure and inspire dishes that will elicit rave reviews from even your most discriminating friends. I know no greater pleasure than watching someone who does not think they are a fan of Indian cooking take their first mouthful of my food. Their faces invariably light up with a smile radiating pure pleasure and surprise. When they ask for my secret, I reply, "the freshly roasted spices and the cooking style, that's all."

The Indian Pantry

ajowan seeds | *wiryali*	cardamom | *elaichi*	fenugreek seeds | *methi dana*
black cumin seeds | *kala jeera*	coriander seeds | *dhania*	mango powder | *amchur*
black onion seeds | *kalonji*	curry leaves | *limro*	poppy seeds | *khus khus*
black mustard seeds | *rai*	fenugreek leaves | *methi patta*	red chili powder | *lal mirch*

FRESH SPICES & HERBS

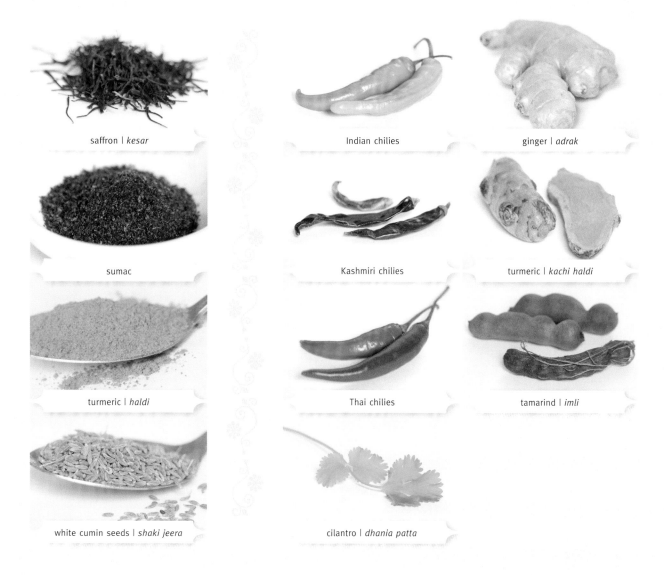

saffron | *kesar*

Indian chilies

ginger | *adrak*

sumac

Kashmiri chilies

turmeric | *kachi haldi*

turmeric | *haldi*

Thai chilies

tamarind | *imli*

white cumin seeds | *shaki jeera*

cilantro | *dhania patta*

FRUITS & VEGETABLES

DAAL

baby eggplant | *ringra*

okra | *bhindi*

mung beans | *mung daal*

cluster beans | *guvar*

unripened papaya | *papeet*

split chickpeas | *chana daal*

drumsticks | *singhu*

white radishes | *mooli*

split red lentils | *masoor daal*

green mango | *kachi keri*

OTHER INGREDIENTS

yellow pigeon peas | *toor daal*

white lentils | *urad daal*

flat rice | *pawa*

asafetida

crispy fried onions | *birista*

clarified butter | *ghee*

chili paste | *sambal olek*

Indian cheese | *paneer*

edible silver foil | *varakh*

cane sugar | *jaggery*

Before You Begin

TO MEASURE BUTTER OR MARGARINE

To measure butter or margarine in a cup, do not melt it and then measure. If the recipe calls for ½ cup (125 mL) of butter or margarine, take a measuring jug and fill with water to the ½ cup (125 mL) level, then add enough solid butter so that the water reaches the 1 cup (250 mL) level. Drain off the water and use the butter as required.

PREPARING CHICKEN

When preparing chicken, always remove the skin and excess fat under the skin and on the flesh. Small chickens are tender and deliciously moist when properly cooked. If you prefer to debone your chicken before adding it to a dish, then go ahead and do it. I prefer to leave it on the bone because the finished dish is more moist. For recipes requiring cut-up chicken, I simply cut right through the bones.

RICE AND BEANS

Always rinse rice before cooking to remove dirt or grit. Then soak it in double the volume of water for half an hour. Change the water once during soaking but not more than twice as rice tends to break easily. Dried beans should be washed twice to remove dust and dirt. Then they should be soaked in fresh water for at least 2 hours. I usually soak my beans overnight as that helps them to cook faster. Do not soak beans for more than 10 hours or they will begin to ferment.

COCONUT MILK

Add coconut milk to curry and bring to a boil over low heat. Once boiling, reduce the heat and bring it to a simmer again. The best flavor is achieved by not overcooking coconut milk, which causes the oil of the coconut milk to surface, changes the flavor and creates an extra greasiness.

YOGURT

For best results, always use plain, unsweetened yogurt that has a slightly sour flavor, unless the recipe specifies otherwise. When adding to curry, bring to a boil slowly, stirring occasionally so yogurt does not curdle and separate. Once it has boiled, the curry may be cooked on slightly high heat if the recipe calls for it.

GHEE OR CLARIFIED BUTTER

Clarified butter can be made by taking margarine and butter in equal proportions and heating over low heat with two pods of cardamom. Heat for at least 1 hour. This will leave the milk solids to settle at the bottom with the clear butter on top. Scoop out as much clear butter as you can. Transfer it into a glass jar and store in the refrigerator for up to 6 months.

THE RIGHT WAY TO DO CHASNI (SUGAR SYRUP)

A concentrated solution of sugar and water is called chasni or sugar syrup. The sugar and water are heated slowly so that the water does not boil before the sugar has dissolved. You must stir gently at this stage. Once all the sugar has dissolved it can be brought to a boil but not stirred.

Chasni has various strengths or degrees. A mild one does not thread when pressed between thumb and forefinger; it just leaves a syrup imprint. The second strength is when the chasni thickens and, when tested between thumb and forefinger, forms one thread. The third strength is when it gives two to three threads. This stage is also known as the soft ball stage. (When a little bit is dropped in cool water the syrup turns into a soft ball.) The last stage is the hard ball, when the syrup almost caramelizes.

SERVING INDIAN FOOD

Eating habits vary drastically across India. Probably no other country in the world has such a variety of foods and eating patterns.

In the North, rice is eaten first with some lentils, then with a chapati and a dry meat dish. In the South, where rice is the staple dish, it is eaten with different coconut-flavored curries. In other places a sweet dish is consumed alongside the rest of the food.

In almost all the recipes, I have noted accompaniments for each particular dish to make your meal as enjoyable as possible.

Bombay Nuts 'n' Bolts (*Chevdo*) 12

Crispy Savory Tidbits (*Nimki*) 14

Paneer Poppers 15

Spicy Indian Cheese (*Paneer Tikka*) 17

Spinach Fritters (*Palak Pakora*) 18

Potato & Onion Fritters (*Alu Piaz Pakora*) 21

Onion Fritters (*Piaz Pakora*) 22

Crispy Lentil-Stuffed Pastries (*Gujarati Kachori*) 23

Arabic-Style Samosas (*Sambosay Arabi*) 26

Sausage Rolls 31

Half-Moon Chicken Pastries 33

Snacks & Appetizers

Bombay Nuts 'n' Bolts

❋ Chevdo

8 cups | 2 L	oil for deep-frying (or enough to fill the skillet ¾ full)
½ lb | 250 g	bag of kettle-fried potato chips
3 cups | 750 mL	chana daal, soaked overnight and drained
2 cups | 500 mL	raw peanuts with skins
3½ cups | 875 mL	thick pawa (see page 13)
1 tsp | 5 mL	black mustard seeds
10	curry leaves
3	green chilies, cut into thin rings (optional)
½ cup | 125 mL	raisins
½ cup | 125 mL	cashew nuts
½ cup | 125 mL	roasted almonds
1 Tbsp | 15 mL	sesame seeds
1 Tbsp | 15 mL	fennel seeds
1 Tbsp | 15 mL	coriander seeds, roasted and cracked
1 tsp | 5 mL	cumin seeds
1 tsp | 5 mL	red chili powder
1 tsp | 5 mL	turmeric
3 Tbsp | 45 mL	sugar
2 tsp | 10 mL	sea salt
½ tsp | 2 mL	citric acid crystals

When friends or visitors arrive at any Gujarati home, they are usually offered a cool drink and snack, and most likely the snack is chevdo. Although there are a lot of variations of chevdo and it can be spiced to your taste, it is always deep-fried and salty. In order to make this, you'll need a large skillet (or a karahi or wok), a small saucepan, two metal sieves and a roll of paper towels. Here I give you the basic recipe and include two variations.

1. Heat the oil in a large, deep skillet (or karahi) over high heat. While the oil is heating, place some paper towels on a large plate or baking dish and pour the bag of potato chips on it. When the oil is hot, fry the chana daal until crispy, about 10 minutes.

2. Remove the chana daal with a slotted spoon, drain in a sieve (placed in a bowl to catch the oil), then place on top of the chips.

3. Add the peanuts to the hot oil and fry for approximately 6–7 minutes. Remove with a slotted spoon and drain in a sieve before placing on top of the daal.

4. Place 1 cup (250 mL) of the flat rice (pawa) into a metal sieve and immerse the sieve in the hot oil. The pawa will immediately puff up and triple in size. Remove from the oil right away and pour into another sieve to drain. Allow to cool.

5. Repeat with the remaining pawa, 1 cup (250 mL) at a time, each time making sure the oil is hot before adding the rice. (If the oil is not hot enough the pawa will not puff up and instead will soak up oil.) Place all the pawa

on top of the peanuts, daal and chips. When cool, place the pawa, peanuts, daal and chips in a large bowl.

6. Drain about ½ cup (125 mL) of the frying oil and put it in a small saucepan over medium-high heat. Fry the mustard seeds for about 30 seconds or until the seeds start to pop. Add the curry leaves and sauté for about 15 seconds. Add the green chilies, if using, and fry until crispy.

7. Add the raisins, cashews and almonds to the saucepan and fry for 1 minute. Drain and add to the chana daal mixture.

8. In a small bowl, combine the sesame seeds, fennel seeds, coriander seeds, cumin seeds, red chili powder and turmeric. Add to the chana daal mixture and use a slotted spoon to toss and mix well.

9. Sprinkle the sugar, salt and citric acid crystals overtop and toss again to mix evenly. Cool to room temperature and store in an airtight container. Chevdo keeps well up to 4 months, but will surely be gone before then—it's very addictive. *Serves 10–12*

TAHERA'S TIPS
Citric acid crystals are a natural preservative that can enhance the flavor of some foods. You can find food-grade citric acid in the baking supplies aisle of your local grocery store or at specialty food stores.

Pawa is a kind of dried, flaked rice that puffs up when fried. You can find it at Indian grocery stores and it is pictured on page 5.

VARIATION 1

Soak 2 cups (500 mL) of whole mung beans in water for one day, tie in a muslin cloth and let sit for another half day, then deep-fry. Follow the recipe for original chevdo, but add the soaked mung beans and ½ cup (125 mL) roasted pine nuts before adding the spices.

VARIATION 2

Instead of potato chips, use potato straws or matchstick-style potato chips. Follow the original chevdo recipe, adding 2 cups (500 mL) of sev noodles (noodles made from chickpea flour, which you can find in Indian grocery stores), ½ cup (125 mL) pistachios and ½ cup (125 mL) chopped dates. Add 1 Tbsp (15 mL) of dried mango powder when adding the salt and citric acid crystals. Toss to mix well.

Crispy Savory Tidbits

❋ *Nimki*

This delicious crispy snack may be prepared and kept for 2–3 weeks in an airtight container. Serve at tea time or with drinks.

2 cups | 500 mL	all-purpose flour
1 tsp | 5 mL	salt
½ tsp | 2 mL	red chili powder
½ tsp | 2 mL	ground cumin
½ tsp | 2 mL	ajowan seeds
1 tsp | 5 mL	black onion seeds
1 tsp | 5 mL	garam masala (see page 173)
3 Tbsp | 45 mL	melted butter or vegetable oil
½ cup | 125 mL	cold water
¼ cup | 60 mL	oil for deep-frying

1. In a large bowl, stir together the flour, salt, red chili powder, ground cumin, ajowan seeds, black onion seeds and garam masala.

2. Add the melted butter and rub it into the flour using your fingers, until it looks like coarse breadcrumbs.

3. Slowly add enough cold water to make a firm dough. Knead for 10 minutes or until the dough is smooth and elastic.

4. Cover and set aside for 30 minutes.

5. Divide the dough into 5–6 balls. On a lightly floured board, roll out each ball until it's about ¼ inch (6 mm) thick. Cut into finger-width strips.

6. Heat the oil in a large, deep skillet (or karahi) over medium-high heat and fry the strips—a few at a time—until golden brown.

7. Remove with a slotted spoon and drain on paper towels.

8. If you like, you can sprinkle more salt and garam masala over the strips before serving. Serve warm, or cool and store in an airtight container. *Serves 6–8*

TAHERA'S TIPS

In this recipe, I use ajowan seeds, which are also known as carom or thymol. They have a bitter, hot bite to them and release a distinctive aroma when crushed. You can find them in Indian grocery stores and they are pictured on page 2.

Paneer Poppers

1. Heat the oil in a saucepan over medium-high heat.

2. Stir in the flour and cook for about 1 minute. Add the milk, a little at a time, stirring continuously.

3. Add the mashed potatoes, red chili powder, pepper, grated paneer and salt. Remove from the heat and let cool.

4. When cool enough to handle, form the batter into 2-inch (5 cm) balls and flatten. It should make 10–15 patties.

5. Roll each patty in breadcrumbs and refrigerate for at least 30 minutes.

6. Heat the oil in a large, deep skillet (or karahi) over medium-high heat. When it's hot, add the coated patties and deep-fry for about 1 minute. Serve hot with daal or a sauce of your choice. *Serves 4–6*

A very popular snack from northern India, this is usually served with tamarind sauce.

¼ cup | 60 mL	vegetable oil
¼ cup | 60 mL	all-purpose flour
1 cup | 250 mL	milk
5	potatoes, boiled and mashed
½ tsp | 2 mL	red chili powder
½ tsp | 2 mL	ground black pepper
7 oz | 200 g	paneer, grated (see page 17)
to taste	salt
1 cup | 250 mL	breadcrumbs
2 cups | 500 mL	oil for deep-frying

Spicy Indian Cheese (facing page)
served with Tomato Chutney (page 164)

Spicy Indian Cheese

❊ *Paneer Tikka*

1. Cut the paneer into strips about 1½ inches long and ¼ inch thick (4 cm × 6 mm).

2. Mix the yogurt, garlic and ginger pastes, ajowan seeds, ground cumin, green chili paste, lemon juice and salt in a large container, combining well.

3. Coat the paneer strips with the spiced yogurt mixture.

4. Heat the oil in a large, deep skillet (or karahi) over high heat.

5. Fry the paneer strips, basting them with the spiced yogurt mixture. Fry for at least 1 minute or until they are just golden brown. Serve with your choice of chutney. *Serves 6*

TAHERA'S TIPS

You can make your own paneer, but it is much easier to buy it already made, especially if you're new to Indian cooking. You can pick it up at any Indian grocery store. If you want to try making it yourself, see the recipe in my first book, *Simply Indian*.

This is a wonderful starter for a festive meal. You can also use this recipe as a delicious garnish for dishes such as Casserole-Style Prawn Pilau (page 98) or Zanzibari Pilau (page 99). My family also enjoys them with Puri (page 147).

4 cups | 1 L	solid paneer
2 Tbsp | 30 mL	plain yogurt
1 tsp | 5 mL	garlic paste (see page 177)
1 tsp | 5 mL	ginger paste (see page 176)
1 tsp | 5 mL	ajowan seeds
1 tsp | 5 mL	ground cumin
½ tsp | 2 mL	green chili paste
2 Tbsp | 30 mL	fresh lemon juice
½ tsp | 2 mL	salt
2 cups | 500 mL	oil for deep-frying

Spinach Fritters

❁ Palak Pakora

Originating from the state of Punjab, these fritters are now a very popular snack all over India. The flavors vary from region to region, but chana flour is always used for the batter. Pakoras are delicious with Date & Tamarind Chutney (page 162) or Red Coconut Chutney (page 163).

2½ cups | 625 mL	chana flour
½ tsp | 2 mL	asafetida (see page 22)
½ tsp | 2 mL	salt
1 tsp | 5 mL	roasted cumin seeds, coarsely ground
1 tsp | 5 mL	coriander seeds, coarsely ground
½ tsp | 2 mL	garlic paste (see page 177)
1	small onion, finely chopped
½ tsp | 2 mL	red chili powder
1½ tsp | 7 mL	fennel seeds, coarsely ground
1 cup | 250 mL	water
¼ tsp | 1 mL	Eno fruit salt (see page 21)
15	whole spinach leaves
2 cups | 500 mL	oil for deep frying

1. In a large bowl, mix together the chana flour, asafetida, salt, cumin and coriander seeds, garlic paste, onion, red chili powder and fennel seeds.

2. Using a tablespoon, add water little by little until the mixture forms a very thick, pasty batter. Add the fruit salt and mix well.

3. Heat the oil in a large, deep skillet (or karahi) over medium-high heat.

4. When the oil is hot, dip the spinach leaves one by one in the batter, ensuring each is well coated. Gently drop the coated leaves in the hot oil and fry, a few at a time, until just golden brown.

5. Remove with a slotted spoon and place on paper towels to drain. Repeat until all the spinach leaves are fried. Serve hot. *Serves 4–6*

VARIATION: PANEER PAKORA

Cut 1 lb (500 g) of solid paneer (see page 17) into cubes about 2 inches square (5 cm × 5 cm) and prepare the batter as above. Dip the cubes in the batter, coating evenly, and deep-fry in the hot oil until golden brown. Remove with a slotted spoon and drain on paper towels. Serve hot.

TAHERA'S TIPS

Chana flour is simply chickpea flour. You might find it sold under other names, including gram flour, garbanzo bean flour, besan flour or ceci flour. I have tried using all-purpose flour as a substitute, but the batter is not as crispy and the taste is not the same. Look for chana flour at Indian grocery stores.

Spinach Fritters (facing page)
served with Raita (page 169)

Potato & Onion Fritters

❋ *Alu Piaz Pakora*

1. In a large bowl, mix together the potatoes, onions, almonds, chana flour, garlic paste, salt, red chili powder, fennel seeds, coriander seeds, cumin seeds, cilantro and black pepper.

2. Using a tablespoon, add the buttermilk little by little until the mixture forms a very thick, pasty batter. Add the fruit salt and mix well.

3. Heat the oil in a large, deep skillet (or karahi) over medium-high heat.

4. When the oil is hot, using a tablespoon, gently drop dumpling-sized portions in the hot oil and fry, a few at a time, until just golden brown.

5. Remove with a slotted spoon and place on paper towels to drain.

6. Repeat until all the batter is gone. Serve hot. *Serves 4–6*

TAHERA'S TIPS

Eno fruit salt is a combination of sodium bicarbonate, citric acid and sodium carbonate. You can pick it up at any Indian grocery store or even any pharmacy. Since it is an antacid, it may seem like an odd ingredient to add, but you can't leave it out! It makes the batter fluffy and light.

A specialty from Punjab, these fritters are very popular starters at weddings in northern India and here in North America too. Serve with Raita (page 169) or with tamarind sauce for dipping.

2	medium potatoes, chopped into ¾-inch (2 cm) cubes
4	medium onions, peeled and thinly sliced
1 cup | 250 mL	slivered almonds
2 cups | 500 mL	chana flour (see page 18)
½ tsp | 2 mL	garlic paste (see page 177)
½ tsp | 2 mL	salt
½ tsp | 2 mL	red chili powder
1 Tbsp | 15 mL	whole fennel seeds
1 Tbsp | 15 mL	coarsely ground coriander seeds
1 Tbsp | 15 mL	coarsely ground cumin seeds
¾ tsp | 4 mL	chopped cilantro
1 tsp | 5 mL	coarsely ground black pepper
1½ cups | 375 mL	buttermilk
¾ tsp | 4 mL	Eno fruit salt
4 cups | 1 L	oil for deep-frying

Onion Fritters

❋ *Piaz Pakora*

Crunchy and scented with cumin and coriander seeds, this popular North Indian snack can also be served with an afternoon tea or drink. I serve it with tamarind chutney and rarely are there any leftovers.

2½ cups | 625 mL	chana flour (see page 18)
½ tsp | 2 mL	asafetida
½ tsp | 2 mL	salt
1 tsp | 5 mL	coarsely ground coriander seeds
1 tsp | 5 mL	coarsely ground cumin seeds
½ tsp | 2 mL	garlic paste (see page 177)
1 cup | 250 mL	water
3	large onions, sliced
½ tsp | 2 mL	fennel seeds
½ tsp | 2 mL	red chili powder
½ cup | 125 mL	chopped cilantro
¼ tsp | 1 mL	Eno fruit salt (see page 21)
4 cups | 1 L	oil for deep-frying

1. In a large bowl, mix together the flour, asafetida, salt, coriander, cumin and garlic paste.

2. Using a tablespoon, add water little by little to form a thick, pasty batter.

3. Add the onions, fennel seeds, red chili powder, cilantro and fruit salt.

4. Heat the oil in a large, deep skillet (or karahi) over medium-high heat.

5. When the oil is hot, using a tablespoon, gently drop dumpling-sized portions in the hot oil and fry, a few at a time, until just golden brown.

6. Remove with a slotted spoon and place on paper towels to drain.

7. Repeat until all the batter is gone. Serve hot. *Serves 4–6*

TAHERA'S TIPS

Asafetida is a spice powder with a strong smell (like that of garlic), but a mild taste. Use it in small amounts in condiments to complement turmeric, cumin and mustard seeds. You can buy it at Indian grocery stores and some large supermarkets.

Crispy Lentil-Stuffed Pastries

※ *Gujarati Kachori*

This spicy snack from Gujarat is usually served as a starter. Round balls of dough are filled with a spiced bean mixture and then fried. They are quite filling but absolutely delicious. Serve them hot with Red Coconut Chutney (page 163). Thank you to my sister-in-law, Rubab Bhabi, for sharing this recipe with me.

FOR THE DOUGH

1. In a small bowl, combine the oil and water.

2. Place the flour in a food processor and add the water and oil mixture to the flour little by little as you blend to make a soft, pliable and elastic dough.

3. Cover and set aside for 2–3 hours.

FOR THE FILLING

1. Place the chana daal in a saucepan and cover with water. Bring to a boil and cook over medium-high heat for about 10 minutes.

2. Add the mung daal and continue to boil for about 8–10 minutes until soft. Drain any excess water, transfer to a large bowl to cool, then mash the daal slightly with a fork, the back of a spoon or your hand.

3. Combine the peas and corn in a microwave-safe bowl and microwave on high for 1–2 minutes. Mash them slightly with a fork, the back of a spoon or your hand. When slightly cool, add to the daal mixture.

(continued on next page)

DOUGH

¼ cup | 60 mL	vegetable oil
¼ cup | 60 mL	water
1½ cups | 375 mL	all-purpose flour

FILLING

½ cup | 125 mL	chana daal (soaked overnight and drained)
¾ cup | 185 mL	mung daal (soaked overnight and drained)
½ cup | 125 mL	frozen peas (thawed)
½ cup | 125 mL	frozen peaches and cream corn (thawed)
1	medium carrot, finely chopped
1 small bunch	green onions, chopped
2	green chilies, chopped
2 Tbsp | 30 mL	vegetable oil
½ tsp | 2 mL	black mustard seeds
½ tsp | 2 mL	fenugreek seeds
6–7	curry leaves
½ tsp | 2 mL	garlic paste (see page 177)
½ tsp | 2 mL	sugar
¼ tsp | 1 mL	asafetida (see page 22)
3 Tbsp | 45 mL	fresh lemon juice

TO FINISH THE PASTRIES

4 cups | 1 L	oil for deep-frying

Make sure to prepare the dough first because it has to sit for 2–3 hours before you can roll it out. These can also be made in advance by partially frying and then freezing them for later use. I have kept them frozen for 4–5 months with no problem.

4. Add the carrot, green onions and green chilies to the daal mixture.

5. Heat the 2 Tbsp (30 mL) of oil in a large, deep skillet (or karahi) over high heat. When hot, add the mustard seeds. When they begin to crackle, add the fenugreek seeds, curry leaves and garlic paste. Give it a quick stir and then add the sugar and asafetida. Stir again and, finally, add the lemon juice.

6. Add the daal mixture to the skillet and fry for at least 3–4 minutes. Transfer to a large bowl to cool.

7. When cool enough to handle, form the mixture into 28–30 golf ball–sized portions. Set on a plate or in a baking dish.

TO FINISH THE KACHORIS

1. Working one by one, pull off a small portion of dough. Stretch the dough ball out slightly and place over a veggie ball. Gently pull the dough around the veggie ball to completely cover it. Seal it tightly all around so the mixture is completely covered.

2. Repeat with the remaining dough and veggie balls.

3. Heat the oil in a large, deep skillet (or karahi) over medium-high heat. Deep-fry until the kachoris are golden brown.

4. Remove with a slotted spoon and drain on paper towels. Serve hot with chutney. *Makes 15–18 pastries*

Bombay Nuts 'n' Bolts
(page 12)

Crispy Lentil-Stuffed Pastries
(page 23)

Arabic-Style Samosas

✳ *Sambosay Arabi*

These delicious bite-sized samosas are very hard to resist. Serve them with a salad (try Tabouli on page 46). Thanks very much to Maryam Kermalli for sharing this wonderful appetizer, which I was dying to make and share with everybody!

DOUGH

3 cups	750 mL	all-purpose flour
¾ tsp	4 mL	sea salt
½ cup	125 mL	margarine
¾ cup	185 mL	water

FILLING

½ lb	250 g	ground beef or lamb
1 tsp	5 mL	garlic paste (see page 177)
½ tsp	2 mL	ginger paste (see page 176)
pinch		red chili powder
¼ tsp	1 mL	sea salt
1 Tbsp	15 mL	chopped mint
1 Tbsp	15 mL	vegetable oil
1		large onion, chopped
3 cups	750 mL	oil for deep-frying

FOR THE DOUGH

1. In a large bowl, combine the flour and salt.

2. Add the margarine and rub it into the flour using your fingers, until it looks like coarse breadcrumbs.

3. Mix in water a little at a time until you have a soft pliable dough. Knead the dough for about 10 minutes, then divide into 6 portions and form each into a ball.

4. Cover with a tea towel and set aside for at least 30 minutes.

FOR THE FILLING

1. Put the ground beef or lamb in a large, deep skillet (or karahi) with the garlic and ginger pastes, red chili powder, salt and chopped mint. Set over medium-high heat, stirring constantly and breaking up lumps. Cook until all the liquid has evaporated and the meat is dry and almost sticks to the pan.

2. Remove the pan from the heat and set aside.

3. In a small saucepan, warm the 1 Tbsp (15 mL) of vegetable oil over medium-high heat. Add the chopped onion and sauté for 2–3 minutes, until it is soft and translucent. Add the onion to the meat mixture, mix well and set aside.

TO MAKE THE SAMOSAS

1. Roll out each ball of dough into a circle about 6 inches (15 cm) in diameter, using more flour to keep it from sticking.

2. Brush 3 of the circles with oil and sprinkle lightly with flour. Place each of the other 3 circles on top of the ones with oil and flour. Press lightly all around to seal them together. Now you have a total of 3 rounds of rolled out circles.

3. On a lightly floured surface roll out each of the 3 rounds even further until they reach a diameter of 14 inches (35 cm).

4. Cut into 2½-inch-wide (6 cm) strips. You should be able to get a total of 4 strips. Place 1½ tsp (7 mL) of filling on one end of a strip of pastry. Fold the pastry

(continued on next page)

TAHERA'S TIPS

If you want to make these samosas the fast and easy way, just pick up a package of samosa wrappers in the freezer section of your local Indian grocery store. They're commonly known as "samosa par."

diagonally over the filling, forming a triangle, then make a straight fold up, followed by another diagonal fold in the opposite direction of the first fold. Continue folding to the end of the strip. Moisten the end of the pastry with water and press to seal. See illustration on pages 26 and 27. Repeat with the remaining strips, placing the finished pastries on a cloth.

5. Heat the oil in a large, deep skillet (or karahi) over high heat. It's ready when the oil reaches a temperature of 375°F (190°C). Cooking 4 or 5 at a time, deep-fry the triangles for about 3 minutes or until they turn golden. Watch that the heat is not too high; if the pastries fry too quickly the inner layer of pastry won't cook before the outside browns.

6. Remove with a slotted spoon and drain on paper towels. Serve with wedges of lemon. *Makes 12 samosas*

Arabic-Style Samosas (page 26)
served with (front to back) Fresh Green Chutney
(page 162) , Date & Tamarind Chutney (page 162),
Tomato Chutney (page 164)

Sausage Rolls (facing page)
served with Tomato Chutney (page 164)

Sausage Rolls

1. For the pastry, sift the flour into a large mixing bowl and add the salt. Mix to combine.

2. Place the margarine on a shallow plate and divide it into four equal parts. Add one-quarter of the margarine to the flour and combine using a pastry cutter.

3. Add the lemon juice and the water a little at a time and mix into a stiff dough using your hands.

4. Roll out the pastry into a rectangular strip and distribute another one-quarter of the margarine in small lumps over two-thirds of the pastry. Fold the strip of pastry into three so that the third without margarine is inside. Seal the ends and press the rolling pin over the pastry to form air pockets.

5. Give the pastry a half-turn and roll it out again into a rectangular strip. Apply another one-quarter of the margarine over two-thirds of the pastry. Fold and roll. Repeat with the final portion of margarine. After the last folding, roll out the pastry once more and fold it again (without any margarine). Now the pastry is ready.

6. For the filling, heat the oil in a large, deep skillet (or karahi) over medium-high heat. Sauté the onions for about 4 minutes. Remove from the skillet and set aside.

7. Wipe any leftover oil in the skillet and add the ground beef, the ginger and garlic pastes, salt and pepper, lemon juice and oregano. Sauté until the beef is cooked through and very dry. Remove from the heat, add the sautéed onions and mix well. Set aside.

(continued on next page)

Sausage rolls are always a popular appetizer. This is a variation that my family just loves. If you're short on time, simply purchase puff pastry at your local grocery store instead of making it from scratch.

FLAKY PASTRY

3 cups | 750 mL	flour
pinch	salt
½ cup | 125 mL	margarine
1 tsp | 5 mL	fresh lemon juice
¾ cup | 185 mL	cold water

FILLING

¼ cup | 60 mL	vegetable oil
2	large onions, finely chopped
1 lb | 500 g	ground beef
1 tsp | 5 mL	garlic paste (see page 177)
1 tsp | 5 mL	ginger paste (see page 176)
1 tsp | 5 mL	salt
1 tsp | 5 mL	ground black pepper
¼ cup | 60 mL	fresh lemon juice
½ tsp | 2 mL	oregano
1	egg, beaten

8. Preheat the oven to 400°F (200°C). Grease a baking sheet.

9. Roll out the pastry into a large square about ¼ inch (6 mm) thick. Cut the pastry into long strips about 3 inches (7.5 cm) wide.

10. Place the meat in the middle of a strip. Brush one edge of the strip with beaten egg and roll over to seal. The seam should be on the bottom of the roll.

11. Cut the roll into small sausage rolls, about 2 inches (5 cm) long. Place them on the greased baking sheet, prick with a fork and bake about 30 minutes. *Makes 12 sausage rolls*

Half-Moon Chicken Pastries

Crunchy and irresistible, these pastries are a fusion of Eastern and Western flavors. The white sauce gives them a creamy filling. Serve with tamarind chutney. Thanks to Tahera Haji for sharing this recipe with me.

FOR THE FILLING

1. Heat the oil in a large, deep skillet (or karahi) over medium-high heat and fry the onions until almost brown.

2. Add the garlic paste, green chili, chicken, salt, pepper and chopped cilantro.

3. Cook until all the liquid has evaporated. Set aside.

FOR THE WHITE SAUCE

1. Melt the butter in a small saucepan over medium heat. Add the flour and stir for about 1 minute, being careful to not let it brown.

2. Add the milk, salt and pepper and cook for at least 5 minutes to make sure the sauce has thickened, stirring occasionally.

3. Add the white sauce over the cooked chicken mixture. Stir to coat and set aside.

(continued on next page)

FILLING

2 Tbsp | 30 mL	vegetable oil
2	medium onions, chopped
½ tsp | 2 mL	garlic paste (see page 177)
1	green chili, chopped
½ lb | 250 g	boneless, skinless chicken breast, cut into bite-sized pieces
½ tsp | 2 mL	salt
½ tsp | 2 mL	ground black pepper
¼ cup | 60 mL	chopped cilantro

WHITE SAUCE

2 Tbsp | 30 mL	butter
¼ cup | 60 mL	all-purpose flour
1 cup | 250 mL	milk
¼ tsp | 1 mL	salt
¼ tsp | 1 mL	ground black pepper

(ingredients continued on next page)

DOUGH

4 cups	1 L	all-purpose flour
2 Tbsp	30 mL	baking powder
3½ cups	875 mL	water
3 Tbsp	45 mL	margarine
1 Tbsp	15 mL	salt

TO MAKE THE PASTRIES

2 cups	500 mL	vegetable oil
1		egg, beaten
½ cup	125 mL	fine breadcrumbs

FOR THE DOUGH

1. In a large bowl, combine the flour and baking powder. Stir well to combine evenly.

2. Heat the water, margarine and salt in a large saucepan. When the water starts to boil, remove from the heat and slowly add the flour to the saucepan, stirring to remove any lumps.

3. Return the saucepan to the stovetop over low heat and mix gently to get a thick, smooth dough. Touch the dough; it should not stick to your fingers. If it does, you may have to add a little more flour. Remove from the saucepan to cool.

4. When the dough is cool enough to handle, roll out to about ⅜ inch (1 cm) thick. Cut into 4-inch (10 cm) rounds with a pastry cutter.

TO MAKE THE PASTRIES

1. Put 1 tsp (5 mL) of filling on each pastry round. Fold in half and pinch the edges to seal the filling inside the pastry.

2. Heat the oil in a large, deep skillet (or karahi) over medium-high heat.

3. Dip each half-moon pastry in the beaten egg and then coat with the breadcrumbs. Fry until golden brown, about 30 seconds on each side. Remove and drain on absorbent paper. *Serves 6*

Half-Moon Chicken Pastries (page 33)
served with Red Coconut Chutney (page 163)

Peppery Tamarind Soup (*Rasam*) 38

Leek Soup with Baby Potatoes & Cilantro 40

Spiced Bean & Cucumber Salad (*Kosumbri*) 41

Spiced Cucumber Salad with Mango (*Modern Kosumbri*) 42

Lebanese Salad 43

Spicy White Radish & Cucumber Salad 44

Tabouli 46

Onion Salad 47

Soups &
Salads

Peppery Tamarind Soup

❈ *Rasam*

The word rasam *simply means "soup" in Tamil, and the word is used to describe a variety of soups all made from a broth of tamarind or tomatoes and spiced with black pepper. This tasty, light soup is always served as a starter for a fabulous, rich meal in southern India. I grew to like this soup so much that I include it as a complement to any south Indian meal.*

½ cup | 125 mL	toor daal, soaked overnight and drained (see page 110)
5 cups | 1.25 L	water
2 Tbsp | 30 mL	tamarind pulp
½ cup | 125 mL	hot water
3	tomatoes, finely chopped
½ tsp | 2 mL	sea salt
2 Tbsp | 30 mL	vegetable oil
1 tsp | 5 mL	mustard seeds
6	curry leaves
½ tsp | 2 mL	ground roasted cumin seeds
2 Tbsp | 30 mL	rasam powder (see page 175)
¼ cup | 60 mL	chopped cilantro

1. Place the daal and 2 cups (500 mL) of the water in a saucepan over medium-high heat. Cook, partially covered, until the daal is completely mushy, about 40 minutes.

2. Meanwhile, soak the tamarind pulp in the ½ cup (125 mL) of hot water for about 10 minutes. Squeeze the pulp and dissolve it in the water. Strain through a sieve, discarding the seeds and fibers.

3. Add the tamarind to the toor daal along with the remaining 3 cups (750 mL) of water. Bring to a boil.

4. Add the tomatoes and salt and return to a boil.

5. Reduce the heat to medium-low and let simmer for 15 minutes, whisking occasionally to purée the soup.

6. Just before serving, temper the soup by heating the oil in a skillet on medium-high heat. Add the mustard seeds. When they start to pop, add the curry leaves, cumin seeds and rasam powder. Stir and immediately pour over the rasam.

7. Stir well, garnish with the cilantro and serve hot. *Serves 6–8*

TAHERA'S TIPS
Tamarind pulp is commonly used in Indian cooking. It has a sour taste and is actually one of the main ingredients in Worcestershire sauce. It comes in different forms—powdered and concentrated paste among them—but the best way to buy it is in pulp form. Simply reconstitute in hot water, press through a fine sieve to remove the seeds and use both the water and the pulp in your recipe.

Leek Soup with Baby Potatoes & Cilantro

Occasionally during the compilation of this book, I had to decide whether to add a recipe or not. This recipe made it in because whenever I make this soup for my family, they always ask for more. Try it out and you'll know what I mean.

¼ cup | 60 mL	vegetable oil
1	large leek, washed and chopped
4–5	baby potatoes cut in half
2	stalks celery, chopped
2	shallots, chopped
2	green onions, chopped
1	large carrot, chopped
1 bunch	parsley, chopped
½ tsp | 2 mL	ground black pepper
1½ cups | 375 mL	water
2 cups | 500 mL	skim milk
1 tsp | 5 mL	garlic paste (see page 177)
½ cup | 125 mL	sour cream
½ cup | 125 mL	chopped cilantro
to taste	salt
2 Tbsp | 30 mL	sour cream (for garnish)

1. Heat the oil in a medium-sized saucepan over medium heat. Sauté the leek for about 3 minutes, then add the potatoes and celery and continue sautéing for another 3 minutes.

2. Add the shallots, green onions, carrot and parsley. Sauté for 5 minutes. Season with the pepper.

3. Add the water and milk and bring to a boil, stirring occasionally. Add the garlic paste, reduce the heat to low and simmer for at least 30 minutes.

4. Remove from the heat and cool slightly, then purée in a blender or food processor.

5. Add the ½ cup (120 mL) of sour cream, stir well and add half the chopped cilantro and the salt.

6. Return to a boil, then serve immediately, garnished with the remaining 2 Tbsp (30 mL) of sour cream and the remaining cilantro. *Serves 4*

Spiced Bean & Cucumber Salad

❋ Kosumbri

The nutritional importance of eating raw vegetables and soaked and softened daal is recognized in most south Indian traditional dinners. This salad combines both of those health benefits. Different versions of raw salads all known as kosumbri are regularly served. This was one of Lord Rama's favorite foods.

½ cup | 125 mL	mung daal, soaked for 2–3 hours and drained
¾ cup | 185 mL	grated fresh coconut
½	English cucumber, finely chopped
2	green chilies, seeded and chopped
½ tsp | 2 mL	sea salt
2 Tbsp | 30 mL	fresh lime juice
1 Tbsp | 15 mL	vegetable oil
1 tsp | 5 mL	black mustard seeds
5	curry leaves

1. In a large bowl, combine the daal, coconut, cucumber, chilies, sea salt and lime juice.

2. Heat the oil in a small saucepan over medium-high heat.

3. When the oil is hot, add the mustard seeds. When the seeds start to pop, add the curry leaves, then immediately pour over the salad. Toss and serve. *Serves 4*

TAHERA'S TIPS
Fresh coconut is best, but if you don't have fresh coconut, you can use ½ cup (125 mL) unsweetened desiccated coconut.

Spiced Cucumber Salad with Mango

✳ Modern Kosumbri

This is just a variation on kosumbri (see previous page), but without the beans. One of those salads that may be served with almost every Indian meal, it's refreshing, light and so easy to put together.

½ cup | 125 mL	grated carrots
½ cup | 125 mL	grated fresh coconut
½ cup | 125 mL	raw mango, diced
1	red onion, thinly sliced
½ cup | 125 mL	chopped cucumber
2 Tbsp | 30 mL	fresh lemon juice
2	green chilies, seeded and chopped
1	tomato, chopped
2 Tbsp | 30 mL	vegetable oil
1 tsp | 5 mL	black mustard seeds
pinch	coarsely ground roasted cumin seeds

1. Combine the carrots, coconut, mango, onion, cucumber, lemon juice, chilies and tomato in a large glass bowl.

2. Heat the oil in a small saucepan over medium-high heat.

3. When the oil is hot, add the mustard seeds. When the seeds start to pop, add the cumin seeds, then immediately pour over the salad. Toss and serve. *Serves 6*

TAHERA'S TIPS
Keep the lid of the pan on hand when adding seeds to hot oil, to prevent losing the seeds when they start to pop.

Replica of a traditional coconut grater

Lebanese Salad

1. Wash the lettuce leaves well, shake off as much moisture as possible, tear them into bite-sized pieces and place in a serving bowl.

2. Wash and slice the tomatoes, cucumber, radishes and green onions and mix them with the lettuce.

3. Wash and chop the parsley and add it to the salad mixture with the mint.

4. Combine the olive oil, sumac, salt and lemon juice in a small bowl and beat thoroughly with a fork.

5. Pour over the salad mixture and let sit for 10 minutes. Add the toasted pita bread cubes just before serving.

Serves 2–4

TAHERA'S TIPS
The tart, sour taste sensation of sumac features highly in Middle Eastern cuisine; you'll find it in dishes from Lebanon, Syria, Turkey, Iran and Iraq. Usually sold as a powder, you can find it in Indian or Middle Eastern grocery stores.

This traditional Lebanese salad is cooling and very versatile. Serve it with dinner or as an appealing appetizer.

10	romaine lettuce leaves
2	tomatoes
1	medium English cucumber
3	radishes
1 bunch	green onions
½ bunch	parsley
2 Tbsp	30 mL	chopped mint
¼ cup	60 mL	olive oil
1 tsp	5 mL	sumac
½ tsp	2 mL	salt
3 Tbsp	45 mL	fresh lemon juice
1	pita bread, cut into cubes and toasted (like croutons)

Spicy White Radish & Cucumber Salad

This spicy and easy-to-make salad is a great accompaniment to any Indian meal or Western barbecue. It's best prepared at the last minute to retain its crunchiness. This recipe uses mooli, which is also known as daikon radish, Japanese radish or winter radish.

1	long English cucumber, sliced
2	mooli, sliced
½ tsp	2 mL	sea salt
¼ tsp	1 mL	red chili powder
2	green chilies, seeded and quartered lengthwise
¼ tsp	1 mL	ground black pepper
½ tsp	2 mL	roasted cumin seeds
¼ tsp	1 mL	roasted sesame seeds
¼ cup	60 mL	fresh lemon juice

1. Arrange the cucumbers and radishes on a flat serving plate.

2. Combine the salt, red chili powder, chilies, pepper, cumin and sesame seeds in a small bowl, then sprinkle over the cucumbers and radishes.

3. Drizzle the salad with lemon juice and serve immediately. *Serves 4–6*

Tabouli

This very popular Lebanese salad can complement any meal. Bulghur is crushed wheat and is also sold as bulgur or burghul.

¾ cup | 185 mL	bulghur wheat
1½ cups | 375 mL	chopped parsley
¾ cup | 185 mL	finely chopped spring onion
2 Tbsp | 30 mL	chopped mint
2	firm Roma tomatoes, cubed
6	lettuce leaves, finely shredded
¼ tsp | 1 mL	salt
¼ cup | 60 mL	fresh lemon juice
¼ cup | 60 mL	olive oil

1. Soak the bulghur in warm water for 45 minutes. Drain through a fine sieve and squeeze out all the water.

2. Place the bulghur in a bowl; add the parsley, onion, mint, tomatoes and lettuce.

3. Add the salt, lemon juice and olive oil.

4. Toss well to combine and serve immediately in small bowls. *Serves 4*

Onion Salad

1. Slice onions very thinly and put into a bowl.

2. Add the chopped mint leaves and celery seeds.

3. Cut the green chilies in very thin rings and add to the above mixture with the salt.

4. Just before serving add the sliced tomatoes and vinegar and toss. Serve with any dish of your choice. *Serves 4–5*

Fresh, tangy and quick to make, this salad complements all dishes.

1	large sweet red onion
2	large sweet white onions
1 Tbsp | 15 mL	chopped fresh mint leaves
1 tsp | 5 mL	celery seeds
2	green chilies (deseeded)
¼ tsp | 1 mL	salt
1	medium tomato (sliced)
½ cup | 120 mL	white vinegar

Chicken Vindaloo (*Murg Vindaloo*) 50

Curried Chicken Kebabs (*Tikka Murg Kebabs*) 51

Chicken in Green Curry (*Hare Masale Ki Murg*) 52

Moroccan Chicken Pie (*Basteeya*) 54

Chicken Karahi 56

Butter Chicken (*Makhani Murg*) 57

Barbecued Chicken on Skewers (*Reshmi Kebabs*) 58

Dhansak Daal 60

Kerala-Style Baked Salmon in Green Chutney 63

Chicken
& Fish

Chicken Vindaloo

 *Murg Vindaloo*

This very spicy dish can be prepared using mutton or beef instead. Keep in mind that although boneless meat is easy to prepare, using meat still on the bone not only enhances the flavor of the dish but also ensures that it stays moist. Serve this dish with Paratha (page 145).

1 tsp | 5 mL	cumin seeds
½ tsp | 2 mL	mustard seeds
¼ tsp | 1 mL	fenugreek seeds
½	cinnamon stick, in two 1-inch (2.5 cm) pieces
8	cardamom pods
12	black peppercorns
1½ tsp | 7 mL	garlic paste (see page 177)
½ tsp | 2 mL	ginger paste (see page 176)
½ cup | 125 mL	white vinegar
2 lb | 1 kg	whole chicken, cut into pieces
6	red chilies
1	fresh turmeric or
½ tsp | 2 mL	turmeric paste (see below)
6 Tbsp | 90 mL	vegetable oil
½ cup | 125 mL	crispy fried onions (see page 57)
3	tomatoes, chopped
to taste	salt
1 Tbsp | 15 mL	sugar

1. In a food processor or coffee grinder, combine the cumin seeds, mustard seeds, fenugreek, cinnamon sticks, cardamom and peppercorns. Grind to a powder. Combine this spice mixture, the garlic and ginger pastes and the vinegar in a bowl.

2. Using your hands or a spoon, rub this vinegar and spice mixture all over the chicken pieces. Place the chicken in a glass dish and marinate for 4 hours in the refrigerator.

3. In a food processor, combine the chilies and turmeric to make a paste. Set aside.

4. Heat the oil in a large saucepan over medium-high heat. Add the crispy fried onions and chopped tomatoes and cook for about 5 minutes.

5. Add the marinated chicken along with any leftover spice mixture and cook for about 5 minutes. Add the salt, cover and reduce to low heat for about 5–8 minutes. Do not add water.

6. Add the reserved chili and turmeric paste and cook until the chicken is cooked through.

7. To finish, add the sugar (to cut down on the tanginess) and a little more vinegar if desired. *Serves 6*

TAHERA'S TIPS
Fresh turmeric is an excellent ingredient that adds a fresh, zippy taste. It looks like fresh ginger but is orange inside. You can find it at Indian grocery stores, as a whole root or in paste form.

Curried Chicken Kebabs

❊ Tikka Murg Kebabs

1. In a large bowl, combine the ground chicken, 1 cup (250 mL) of the breadcrumbs, grated onion, cilantro, garlic and ginger pastes, garam masala, chaat masala, green chili, red chili powder, cumin and sea salt.

2. Using your hands, knead the mixture well, about 10 minutes, or until the mixture is smooth and sticky.

3. Divide the mixture into 12 equal portions, shaping each portion into a ball. Flatten the balls into patties that are about 3½ inches (8 cm) in diameter.

4. Heat the oil in a large, deep skillet (or karahi) over medium-high heat. Meanwhile, beat the egg in a shallow dish, and place the remaining ½ cup (125 mL) of breadcrumbs into another shallow dish. Dip each kebab into the beaten egg, then into the breadcrumbs to coat. Gently place it in the frying pan and fry until it is a deep golden brown, about 4–5 minutes on each side. Remove the kebabs from the frying pan and drain on paper towels.

5. Serve hot with rice. *Serves 6*

TAHERA'S TIPS

I don't normally deseed green chilies, but you can if you want to make the dish less spicy.

This delicately spiced dish comes from the state of Hyderabad, but it is popular in Delhi and Rajasthan too. These crisp kebabs are great as a starter, but can also be served as a main course with any chutney, a daal and rice.

1½ lb | 750 g	ground chicken
1½ cups | 375 mL	breadcrumbs
1	large onion, grated
½ bunch	cilantro, finely chopped
1½ tsp | 7 mL	garlic paste (see page 177)
1 tsp | 5 mL	ginger paste (see page 176)
1 tsp | 5 mL	garam masala (see page 173)
1 tsp | 5 mL	chaat masala (see page 175)
1	green chili, finely chopped
¼ tsp | 1 mL	red chili powder (optional)
1 tsp | 5 mL	roasted ground cumin seeds
¾ tsp | 4 mL	sea salt
1	egg
1 cup | 250 mL	vegetable oil

Chicken in Green Curry

✳ Hare Masale Ki Murg

This is a rich yet delicate dish with a rather unusual combination of flavors. Serve it at a weekend luncheon or family get-together. Serve with rice, Naan (page 143) or Roti (page 144).

¼ cup | 60 mL	vegetable oil
3	large onions, chopped
4	green chilies
1 bunch	mint
1 bunch	cilantro
1 cup | 250 mL	cashew nuts
1 Tbsp | 15 mL	garlic paste (see page 177)
1 Tbsp | 15 mL	ginger paste (see page 176)
½ cup | 125 mL	plain yogurt
2 lb | 1 kg	chicken, cut into bite-sized pieces
3 Tbsp | 45 mL	ghee or vegetable oil
¼ tsp | 1 mL	turmeric
to taste	salt
1½ cups | 375 mL	warm water
½	cinnamon stick, in two 1-inch (2.5 cm) pieces
2–3	whole cloves
4	cardamom pods
8	black peppercorns
1 tsp | 5 mL	cumin seeds
2 tsp | 10 mL	coriander seeds
2 Tbsp | 30 mL	whipping cream (35%)

1. Heat the oil in a skillet over medium-high heat. Add the onions and sauté until soft. Remove from the heat and set aside.

2. In a food processor, or using a mortar and pestle, grind the green chilies, mint, cilantro, cashews and sautéed onions to make a thick masala paste.

3. In a large bowl, combine this masala paste with the garlic and ginger pastes and the yogurt. Add the chicken and toss with a spoon or rub the paste into the meat using your fingers (this gives it more taste), making sure that the chicken is evenly coated.

4. Heat the ghee or vegetable oil in a large, deep skillet (or karahi) over medium-high heat and add the chicken.

5. Sauté until the ghee or oil separates from the rest of the mixture. Then add the turmeric (this will burn if you add it any earlier) and salt to taste. Continue cooking for about 5 more minutes.

6. Add the water and cook for about 15 minutes, or until the chicken is almost cooked through.

7. Meanwhile, in a food processor or coffee grinder, grind the cinnamon sticks, cloves, cardamom pods, black peppercorns, cumin and coriander seeds.

8. Add this ground spice mix and the cream to the chicken curry. Simmer for another 3–5 minutes. The gravy should be rich and thick. *Serves 4*

Moroccan Chicken Pie

❈ Basteeya

2 Tbsp | 30 mL	olive oil
1	large onion, chopped
2 cloves	garlic, chopped
1	small Thai chili, chopped
½	cinnamon stick (2 inches/5 cm)
1 tsp | 5 mL	good-quality Madras curry powder
1 tsp | 5 mL	finely chopped fresh ginger
1 Tbsp | 15 mL	lemon zest
1 lb | 500 g	ground chicken
2	pitted prunes, finely chopped
¼ cup | 60 mL	spicy green olives, pitted and diced
½ cup | 125 mL	chicken stock
2 Tbsp | 30 mL	fresh lemon juice
¼ tsp | 1 mL	sea salt
½ tsp | 2 mL	ground black pepper
½ cup | 125 mL	chopped green onions
¼ cup | 60 mL	whole toasted almonds
1 tsp | 5 mL	ground cinnamon
5 Tbsp | 75 mL	melted butter or olive oil
8–10	phyllo sheets
1	egg, lightly beaten
2 Tbsp | 30 mL	chopped coriander leaves

In this incredible Moroccan phyllo pie I've created a fusion of Middle East and Eastern flavors. Cinnamon and almonds hidden between the layers of phyllo and the savory chicken filling combine to make a truly delicious dish. There are a lot of ingredients, but they are essential to create that delicate balance of sweet and salty. This recipe doesn't offer too much room for improvisation, but the flavors are definitely daring and it has been very popular in my classes.

1. In a large, deep skillet (or karahi) heat the olive oil over medium-high heat. Sauté the onion until soft, about 5 minutes.

2. Add the garlic, chili, cinnamon stick, curry powder, ginger and lemon zest and sauté for 2 minutes.

3. Stir in the chicken, prunes, olives, chicken stock, lemon juice, salt and pepper. Bring to a boil.

4. Reduce the heat to low and cover. Simmer, without stirring, for 10 minutes.

5. Remove the lid and simmer for a further 5 minutes, or until the liquid has evaporated.

6. Let cool completely, then add the chopped green onions and mix well.

7. Meanwhile, pulse the almonds in a food processor until coarsely chopped. Mix with the ground cinnamon and set aside.

8. Preheat the oven to 375°F (190°C). Brush a 10-inch (25 cm) pie plate with some of the melted butter.

9. Arrange a sheet of phyllo on your work surface, keeping the remaining phyllo under a damp tea towel. Brush the phyllo sheet with melted butter. Place in the middle of the pie plate, allowing the excess phyllo to hang over the edge. Repeat with 4 more sheets of phyllo.

10. Stir the beaten egg and coriander into the chicken mixture. Spoon the mixture into the pie plate. Fold the overhanging phyllo pieces into the middle of the pie one at a time, sprinkling some of the almond mixture between each layer.

11. Butter another piece of phyllo and sprinkle it with some almond mixture. Place over the filling and tuck in the overhang. Repeat with the remaining phyllo sheets and almond mixture.

12. Bake for 20 minutes, or until the top is browned and crisp. Let stand for 5 minutes before cutting into wedges. *Serves 6*

Chicken Karahi

The word karahi *refers to the two-handled Indian frying pan in which this dish is prepared. But it can also be prepared in a wok or any other large, deep saucepan. Here I provide two different ways to make it. The first version is a semidry, delicate dish that derives its flavor from the onion seeds, yogurt and crushed cumin seeds. I recommend you try it for a wonderful weekend luncheon or family get-together. Serve with rice.*

2	boneless chicken breasts, cut into bite-sized pieces
1 tsp | 5 mL	ginger paste (see page 176)
1 tsp | 5 mL	garlic paste (see page 177)
¼ cup | 60 mL	vegetable oil
1 cup | 250 mL	crispy fried onions (see page 57)
3 Tbsp | 45 mL	dried fenugreek leaves
½ tsp | 2 mL	turmeric
1 tsp | 5 mL	black cumin seeds
1 tsp | 5 mL	crushed onion seeds
1 tsp | 5 mL	chili paste (sambal olek)
¾ tsp | 4 mL	sea salt
1 cup | 250 mL	plain yogurt
1 cup | 250 mL	crushed tomatoes
½ cup | 125 mL	water
3 Tbsp | 45 mL	chopped cilantro

1. Wash the chicken and mix well with the ginger and garlic pastes in a glass bowl or container. Marinate in the refrigerator for 1 hour.

2. Heat the oil in a large saucepan (or karahi, if you have one) over medium-high heat, then add the crispy fried onions and stir for 20 seconds (do not let the onions become too dark in color).

3. Add the fenugreek leaves and fry for 1 minute, then add the marinated chicken. Cook, stirring occasionally, for 3–4 minutes.

4. Add the turmeric, black onion seeds, cumin seeds, chili paste, salt and yogurt. Continue cooking for about 2 minutes, then add the crushed tomatoes. Cook for another 2–3 minutes, stirring constantly to keep the mixture from sticking to the pan.

5. Gradually add the water and let simmer for approximately 10 minutes. Garnish with cilantro. *Serves 4–6*

Butter Chicken

❋ Makhani Murg

1. Prick the chicken pieces with a fork and set aside. Combine the ginger and garlic pastes, red chili powder, turmeric, tandoori powder and salt in a small bowl. Rub this mixture into the chicken and let sit for 30 minutes in the refrigerator.

2. In a large, deep saucepan, melt 2 Tbsp (30 mL) of the ghee (clarified butter) over medium-high heat. Add the crispy fried onions and the chicken. Sauté until the chicken is golden brown, about 5–8 minutes. Add the 1 cup (250 mL) of warm water and simmer for 15 minutes, or until chicken is tender.

3. Meanwhile, heat the remaining 4 Tbsp (60 mL) of ghee (clarified butter) in a skillet over medium-high heat. Add the raisins and blanched almonds, sauté for 1 minute, then set aside.

4. Add the 1 cup (250 mL) of thickened milk to the chicken and cook, uncovered, on low heat until the milk is mostly absorbed. Add the Worcestershire sauce, sugar, cardamom and nutmeg.

5. Add the whipping cream, and the reserved raisins and almonds. Bring to a boil and then remove from heat. Serve. *Serves 6*

TAHERA'S TIPS
Crispy fried onions are sold in packages in many supermarkets and Indian grocery stores. You can make them yourself by thinly slicing onions, then deep-frying them until they turn golden brown. Drain them on a paper towel and cool. They will keep in an airtight container for up to 8 months.

This rich Moghlai dish is perhaps the most popular Indian dish among non-Indian North Americans. It is certainly very popular in my advanced cooking classes. Once you try this version, it's going to be your favorite too. Serve with rice and Naan (page 143).

2 lb | 1 kg	chicken pieces
1 tsp | 5 mL	ginger paste (see page 176)
1 tsp | 5 mL	garlic paste (see page 177)
½ tsp | 2 mL	red chili powder
¼ tsp | 1 mL	turmeric
1 Tbsp | 15 mL	tandoori powder (see page 176)
¾ tsp | 4 mL	salt
6 Tbsp | 90 mL	ghee (clarified butter)
¼ cup | 60 mL	crispy fried onions
1 cup | 250 mL	warm water
½ cup | 125 mL	raisins
¼ cup | 60 mL	blanched almonds
4 cups | 1 L	milk, boiled down to 1 cup (250 mL)
1½ Tbsp | 22 mL	Worcestershire sauce
2 tsp | 10 mL	sugar
½ tsp | 2 mL	ground cardamom
½ tsp | 2 mL	ground nutmeg
¾ cup | 185 mL	whipping cream (35%)

Barbecued Chicken on Skewers

✳ Reshmi Kebabs

This popular North Indian dish is delicious and simple to make. It's often served as an appetizer, but to make it into a light meal, serve it with a salad; for a more substantial meal, include Naan (page 143). Instead of using curry masala paste, you could use premade Kashmiri masala paste, which is available in Indian stores.

2 lb | 1 kg	boneless, skinless chicken breast
¼ cup | 60 mL	fresh lemon juice
¾ tsp | 4 mL	salt
½ cup | 125 mL	plain yogurt
1 tsp | 5 mL	ginger paste (see page 176)
1 tsp | 5 mL	garlic paste (see page 177)
2 Tbsp | 30 mL	curry masala paste (see page 174)
2 Tbsp | 30 mL	fresh lemon juice
¼ tsp | 1 mL	orange food coloring (optional)
2 Tbsp | 30 mL	green mango, finely grated
¼ cup | 60 mL	vegetable oil

1. Cut the chicken into 1-inch (2.5 cm) cubes. Place the chicken in a large glass bowl.

2. Pour the ¼ cup (60 mL) of lemon juice over the chicken and sprinkle with the salt. Refrigerate for 1 hour.

3. In a medium bowl, combine the yogurt, ginger and garlic pastes, curry masala paste, the 2 Tbsp (30 mL) of lemon juice, orange food coloring (if using) and green mango.

4. Pour the yogurt mixture over the chicken pieces, making sure all the pieces are well coated. Marinate in the refrigerator for at least 4 hours.

5. Thread the marinated chicken on metal skewers. Brush with the oil, using a pastry brush.

6. Heat the barbecue to medium-high. Grill the kebabs for at least 20 minutes, until the meat is thoroughly cooked and the surface has brown flecks. Serve immediately.
Serves 4

LEFT TO RIGHT
Barbecued Chicken on Skewers (facing page),
Mogul Hamburgers (page 67),
Raita (page 169)

Dhansak Daal

A Parsi specialty cooked on special occasions. If you like, you can substitute mutton for the chicken in this recipe.

¼ cup ǀ 60 mL	toor daal (see page 110)
¼ cup ǀ 60 mL	urad daal
½ cup ǀ 125 mL	chana daal
½ cup ǀ 125 mL	masoor daal
2 lb ǀ 1 kg	chicken, cut into bite-sized pieces
1 tsp ǀ 5 mL	ginger paste (see page 176)
1 tsp ǀ 5 mL	garlic paste (see page 177)
¼ cup ǀ 60 mL	chopped mint
2	green chilies, chopped
½ tsp ǀ 2 mL	turmeric
½ tsp ǀ 2 mL	ground black pepper
8 cups ǀ 2 L	water
3 Tbsp ǀ 45 mL	ghee or vegetable oil
2–3 medium	potatoes, chopped
2 medium	tomatoes, chopped
2 medium	eggplant, peeled and chopped
1 medium	sweet potato, peeled and chopped (optional)

1. Combine the 4 types of daal in a large bowl, cover with cold water and soak overnight, or for at least 3–4 hours. Drain.

2. Place the chicken in a large saucepan. Add the ginger and garlic pastes, chopped mint, chopped green chilies, turmeric and black pepper. Add the drained daal.

3. Add the 8 cups (2 L) of water and let everything cook over medium-high heat for about 15–20 minutes. When the chicken is tender and cooked through, remove it from the saucepan and set aside.

4. Add the potatoes, tomatoes, eggplant and sweet potato (if using) and let cook for 15–20 minutes or until the potatoes are cooked through, stirring occasionally.

5. Grind the daal and vegetable mixture in a blender, but don't purée completely. Return the mixture to the saucepan and add the cooked chicken.

6. For the masala, combine the Kashmiri chilies, cumin seeds, black pepper, coconut, turmeric and salt in a small bowl. Set aside.

7. Heat the oil over medium-high heat in a separate skillet. Add the chopped onion and ginger and garlic pastes and sauté for 2–3 minutes. Then add the spice mixture and cook for another 2–3 minutes. Add this masala mixture to the daal and meat mixture.

8. Add the garam masala and lemon juice and let simmer for a while, about 10–15 minutes. Add water if it is too thick, and cook for a little longer until heated through.

9. Garnish with cilantro and serve with roti, paratha or rice. *Serves 8–10*

TAHERA'S TIPS

Kashmiri chilies are dried red chilies from the valley of Kashmir. They are sold in packets at Indian grocery stores.

MASALA

1 tsp | 5 mL	ground Kashmiri chilies
1 tsp | 5 mL	crushed cumin seeds
1 tsp | 5 mL	ground black pepper
1 Tbsp | 15 mL	unsweetened desiccated coconut
½ tsp | 2 mL	turmeric
to taste	salt
3 Tbsp | 45 mL	vegetable oil
3	medium onions, chopped
1½ tsp | 7 mL	ginger paste (see page 176)
1½ tsp | 7 mL	garlic paste (see page 177)
1 tsp | 5 mL	garam masala (see page 173)
1 Tbsp | 15 mL	fresh lemon juice
½ bunch	cilantro, chopped
1 Tbsp | 15 mL	salt

Kerala-Style Baked Salmon in Green Chutney

1. Wash the fish, sprinkle with the salt and pour the lemon juice over it. Refrigerate for at least 1 hour.

2. Preheat the oven to 400°F (200°C).

3. Combine the green chutney and sour cream in a bowl, mixing well.

4. Lay the fish flat in a large wide casserole dish, and pour the chutney mixture overtop. Make sure the fish is coated with the mixture.

5. Stuff some of the mixture inside the cavity of the fish.

6. Bake for about 25–30 minutes.

7. Remove from the oven and test to see if it is cooked. (If the fish flakes easily in the thickest part, it is done.) Serve immediately. *Serves 6*

Originating from the states of Karnataka and Kerala, this dish has a rich texture and taste but makes a simple meal because it is so easily prepared. It is one of my favorite dishes because of its fresh taste and aroma. Serve it on a bed of steamed rice or with buttered peas, peaches and cream corn and some baked new potatoes. Use fresh fish to make this dish, if possible, as it has more flavor than frozen fish.

1	3 lb (1.5 kg) fresh salmon
1 tsp | 5 mL	sea salt
½ cup | 125 mL	fresh lemon juice
1 cup | 250 mL	fresh green chutney (see page 162)
½ cup | 125 mL	sour cream

Tender Beef Skewers (*Pursindah Sekhi Kebabs*) 66

Mogul Hamburgers (*Chapli Kebabs*) 67

Lacey Kebabs (*Jhali Kebabs*) 69

Galawati Kebab 70

Baked Beef Kebabs (*Dum Ke Kebabs*) 72

Bihari Beef Kebabs 73

Macaroni Meat Pie 74

Crispy Meatballs (*Kali Kebabs*) 77

Lamb Palak 78

Lamb Korma 80

Kashmiri Lamb Curry 81

Beef &
Lamb

Tender Beef Skewers

✳ Pursindah Sekhi Kebabs

This kebab specialty was once popular all over northern India. Variations of the pursindah are now widespread in Iran, Afghanistan and Pakistan. You can use any lean meat, including beef tenderloin, lamb or boneless chicken breast. The meat is cut and flattened into long strips, making the cooking quick if good-quality meat is used. This is an excellent barbecue dish.

3 lb | 1.5 kg	beef tenderloin
3 Tbsp | 45 mL	plain yogurt
1 tsp | 5 mL	garlic paste (see page 177)
1 tsp | 5 mL	ginger paste (see page 176)
1 Tbsp | 15 mL	tandoori powder (see page 176)
1–2	green chilies, finely chopped
¼ cup | 60 mL	onion purée (see page 177)
½ tsp | 2 mL	sea salt
½ tsp | 2 mL	crushed saffron threads
3 Tbsp | 45 mL	vegetable oil

1. Wash the beef and cut into 10 strips, each approximately 3 × 6 inches (7.5 × 15 cm) long. Using a mallet or meat tenderizer, flatten each strip of meat to about ¼-inch (6 mm) thickness. Each strip should be at least 8 inches long when flattened.

2. Run a skewer through each strip of meat so the meat forms an "S" shape on the skewer. Try to use metal skewers because they won't burn on the grill. If you don't have any, make sure to soak wooden skewers for an hour or two first. Place all the beef skewers in a large glass baking pan or baking sheet.

3. In a medium glass bowl, combine the yogurt, garlic and ginger pastes, tandoori powder, chilies, onion purée, sea salt, saffron and vegetable oil. Mix well.

4. Coat the skewered beef strips with the marinade and refrigerate for at least 2 hours.

5. Heat the barbecue to medium-high and place the meat on the grill, pour the remaining marinade over them. Grill until the meat is cooked through and has dark brown grill marks, about 7–8 minutes. Serve immediately with a salad or baked potatoes. *Serves 6*

Mogul Hamburgers

❋ Chapli Kebabs

1. Put the ground meat in a large glass bowl.

2. Add the onions, green chilies, cilantro, mint, nutmeg, black pepper, garlic and ginger pastes and salt, and mix thoroughly with your hands.

3. Marinate the meat for 2 hours in the refrigerator.

4. Form into 6 flat patties and brush with oil.

5. Heat the barbecue to high and cook the patties for 6–10 minutes, turning once, until the surface has dark brown flecks and the meat is cooked through. *Makes 6 patties*

A very popular Indo-Pakistani Mogul classic, these kebabs can also be made ahead of time, frozen and used later. They can be served in hamburger buns or with Naan (page 143) and a simple green salad.

1 lb | 500 g	lean ground lamb or beef
2	medium onions, finely chopped
2	long green chilies, finely chopped
¼ cup | 60 mL	chopped cilantro
2 Tbsp | 30 mL	chopped mint
½ tsp | 2 mL	ground nutmeg
1 Tbsp | 15 mL	ground black pepper
1 Tbsp | 15 mL	garlic paste (see page 177)
1 Tbsp | 15 mL	ginger paste (see page 176)
1 tsp | 5 mL	salt
¼ cup | 60 mL	vegetable oil

TOP TO BOTTOM
Baked Beef Kebabs
(page 72),
Lacey Kebabs
(facing page),
Crispy Meatballs (page 77)

Lacey Kebabs

❋ *Jhali Kebabs*

1. Soak the bread in water for about 2 minutes, then squeeze through a fine sieve (make sure you squeeze out as much water as you can). Put the soaked bread into a large bowl and add the ground beef.

2. Add the chopped chili, cilantro, green onions, garlic and ginger pastes, salt, garam masala and chaat masala to the soaked bread. Using your hands, knead the mixture until thoroughly combined and roll into 1-inch (2.5 cm) balls. Flatten each ball between your palms to form a small patty.

3. Heat the oil in a large, deep skillet (or karahi) over medium-high heat. Put the breadcrumbs in a shallow dish and the eggs in another shallow dish.

4. Dip each kebab into the breadcrumbs, then into the beaten egg. Place them in the skillet gently and fry until they are a deep golden brown, about 2 minutes on each side. Remove the kebabs from the frying pan and drain on paper towels. Serve hot. *Serves 10*

This is a very popular kebab in Pakistan. If you want extra heat, add 2–3 green chilies. I love to serve this with Red Coconut Chutney (page 163), a few lemon wedges and warm Naan (page 143).

9 slices	day-old bread
1½ lb | 750 g	extra lean ground beef
1	green chili, finely chopped with seeds
½ bunch	cilantro, finely chopped
1 bunch	green onions, finely chopped
1½ tsp | 7 mL	garlic paste (see page 177)
1 tsp | 5 mL	ginger paste (see page 176)
½ tsp | 2 mL	sea salt
1 tsp | 5 mL	garam masala (see page 173)
1 tsp | 5 mL	chaat masala (see page 175)
1½ cups | 375 mL	breadcrumbs
2	eggs, beaten
1 cup | 250 mL	vegetable oil (for frying)

Galawati Kebab

This is a recipe from Uttar Pradesh in India. I was enchanted from the very first spoonful when I tasted it at my friend's house. It is a kind of soft meatloaf that just melts in your mouth; the long marinating time achieves tender results. Even though this is a "kebab" recipe, I like to prepare it by just making a meat "paste." If you like, you can form it into patties and bake.

2 lb | 1 kg	ground beef
2 tsp | 10 mL	grated green papaya
1½ tsp | 7 mL	garam masala (see page 173)
1 Tbsp | 15 mL	garlic paste (see page 177)
1 Tbsp | 15 mL	ginger paste (see page 176)
¾ tsp | 4 mL	salt
1 tsp | 5 mL	ground cumin
1 tsp | 5 mL	ground coriander
1 cup | 250 mL	plain yogurt
¾ tsp | 4 mL	red chili powder
3 Tbsp | 45 mL	chana flour (see page 18)
1 Tbsp | 15 mL	finely chopped mint
1 cup | 250 mL	crispy fried onions (see page 57)
2 drops	kewra essence (see page 210)

1. Put the ground beef in a large glass bowl. Add the green papaya, garam masala, garlic and ginger pastes, salt, cumin, coriander, yogurt and red chili powder. Mix well and refrigerate for 24 hours.

2. Preheat the oven to 350°F (180°C).

3. Dry-roast the chana flour in a large, deep skillet (or karahi) over medium-high heat, stirring continuously until the flour turns a light golden brown and develops a toasty fragrance. Sprinkle this flour over the marinated meat mixture.

4. Add the mint, crispy fried onions and kewra essence and mix well.

5. Place the meat mixture in an 11- × 7-inch (2 L) casserole dish and bake for 1½ hours, stirring every 15 minutes until it is a rich brown in color and cooked through.

6. Garnish with thinly sliced sweet onion and wedges of lemon. Serve with roti, naan or any other bread. *Serves 6*

 TAHERA'S TIPS
Make sure to use my recipe for homemade garam masala here—the store-bought version just won't give you the same results.

Baked Beef Kebabs

✳ Dum Ke Kebabs

This is a delightful, tasty Hyderbadi-style dish that I associate with pleasurable family picnics. I always serve it with chutney and salad.

1½ lb | 725 g	sirloin tip beef
1 cup | 250 mL	plain yogurt
1½ Tbsp | 22 mL	ground almonds
¼ cup | 60 mL	vegetable oil
3 Tbsp | 45 mL	pounded green papaya
1 Tbsp | 15 mL	garlic paste (see page 177)
1 Tbsp | 15 mL	ginger paste (see page 176)
1 Tbsp | 15 mL	fennel seeds
1 Tbsp | 15 mL	cumin seeds
1 tsp | 5 mL	coriander seeds
1 tsp | 5 mL	black onion seeds
1 Tbsp | 15 mL	poppy seeds
1 tsp | 5 mL	ground black pepper
1 Tbsp | 15 mL	cardamom pods
1 tsp | 5 mL	whole cloves
1 Tbsp | 15 mL	chana flour (see page 18)
1 tsp | 5 mL	sea salt
½ tsp | 2 mL	saffron threads
½ tsp | 2 mL	garam masala (see page 173)
2	green chilies, pounded with a mortar and pestle
1 cup | 250 mL	crispy fried onions (see page 57)
1 Tbsp | 15 mL	chopped cilantro

1. Wash the beef and cut it into small cubes. Place in a glass bowl.

2. In a separate bowl, combine the yogurt, ground almonds, vegetable oil, papaya and garlic and ginger pastes and mix well. Pour over beef cubes, tossing to coat. Marinate in the refrigerate for 1 hour.

3. Heat a skillet over medium-high heat and dry-roast the fennel seeds, cumin seeds, coriander seeds, black onion seeds, poppy seeds, black pepper, cardamom pods and cloves for 4 minutes. Grind to a fine powder in a food processor or mortar and pestle. Add the spice powder to the marinating meat and stir to coat.

4. Add the chana flour to the same skillet over low heat and dry-roast for 1 minute. Then add the roasted chana flour, sea salt, saffron threads, garam masala, green chilies and half of the crispy fried onions to the marinated meat. Mix well and marinate in the refrigerator for another hour.

5. Preheat the oven to 350°F (180°C). Pour the meat mixture into a large baking dish and bake for 1½–2 hours, until the meat is cooked but still tender and all the juices have evaporated.

6. Using a fork, pull the meat apart. Put into a serving dish and garnish with the rest of the crispy fried onions and chopped cilantro. Serve rolled up in a roti or tortilla.

Serves 8

Bihari Beef Kebabs

1. Cut the meat into strips about 4 × 1 inches (10 × 2.5 cm) and place in a glass dish.

2. Place the chilies, garlic and ginger pastes, cinnamon, turmeric, cardamom, poppy seeds, cumin seeds, pepper and chana daal in a blender and grind.

3. Combine the spice mixture with the yogurt and mix well. Pour over the meat strips and stir to make sure all the meat is coated.

4. Marinate the meat in the refrigerator for 4–5 hours.

5. Preheat the barbecue to high and thread the marinated meat onto metal skewers.

6. Grill the skewers until the meat is tender and the surface has dark brown flecks, about 8–10 minutes.

7. Garnish with the red and white onion rings and serve immediately. *Serves 4*

These succulent morsels of spicy beef are the specialty of the Bihar region of Pakistan. The marinade is accented with cardamom and poppy seeds. Serve these kebabs with Paratha (page 145) or Naan (page 143) and Date & Tamarind Chutney (page 162).

2 lb | 1 kg	beef tenderloin
2	green chilies
2 tsp | 10 mL	garlic paste (see page 177)
1½ tsp | 7 mL	ginger paste (see page 176)
1 tsp | 5 mL	ground cinnamon
¾ tsp | 4 mL	ground turmeric
¾ tsp | 4 mL	ground cardamom
1½ tsp | 7 mL	poppy seeds
2 tsp | 10 mL	roasted cumin seeds, coarsely ground
1 tsp | 5 mL	ground black pepper
1 Tbsp | 15 mL	chana daal
½ cup | 125 mL	plain yogurt
1	medium red onion, cut into rings
1	medium white onion, cut into rings

Macaroni Meat Pie

PASTA

1 lb | 500 g	elbow macaroni
1 tsp | 5 mL	salt
1 Tbsp | 15 mL	olive oil

MEAT SAUCE

¼ cup | 60 mL	olive oil
2	large onions, finely chopped
1 tsp | 5 mL	garlic paste (see page 177)
1¼ lb | 625 g	extra lean ground beef
¼ cup | 60 mL	tomato paste
½ cup | 125 mL	water
2 tsp | 10 mL	oregano
1 tsp | 5 mL	celery seeds
¼ cup | 60 mL	chopped fresh parsley
½ tsp | 2 mL	salt
1 tsp | 5 mL	ground black pepper

WHITE SAUCE

¼ cup | 60 mL	olive oil
5 Tbsp | 75 mL	all-purpose flour
3 cups | 750 mL	milk
½ tsp | 2 mL	salt
½ cup | 125 mL	shredded mozzarella cheese
½ tsp | 2 mL	oregano
½ tsp | 2 mL	ground black pepper
1	egg, lightly beaten
¼ cup | 60 mL	mozzarella cheese, shredded

This is the dish I serve on Friday night (beginning of the weekend). My son Zuber just loves it and is usually the last to leave the dinner table. Try it and you'll know what I mean. The Greek influence shows in the spices listed below; this is not a traditional Indian dish!

1. Bring a large pot of water to a boil, and add the salt, olive oil and macaroni. Cook until al dente, usually about 12–15 minutes. Drain in a colander and rinse with cold water to prevent sticking. Set aside.

2. For the meat sauce, heat the olive oil in a large, deep skillet (or karahi) over medium-high heat. Add the onions and sauté for 2–3 minutes, then add the garlic paste and fry for about 30 seconds.

3. Add the ground beef and cook until the meat begins to brown, stirring well to break up any clumps. Stir in the tomato paste and water, and cook for another 3–4 minutes.

4. Add the oregano, celery seeds, chopped parsley, salt and black pepper, cover and simmer over low heat for 20 minutes.

5. For the white sauce, heat the olive oil in a large saucepan over medium-high heat. Add the flour, fry for approximately 1 minute (be careful not to brown), then slowly add 2½ cups (625 mL) of the milk, stirring continuously.

(continued on page 76)

Add the remaining milk if the sauce is very thick. Add salt, cheese, oregano and black pepper and continue stirring for at least 5 minutes until the sauce has thickened.

6. Preheat oven to 350°F (180°C).

7. Pour the meat sauce in a 9- × 13-inch (3.5 L) casserole dish. Layer the macaroni over the meat sauce. Pour the white sauce over top to cover the macaroni.

8. Pour the beaten egg over the top and then sprinkle with the mozzarella cheese.

9. Bake for 30–40 minutes or until golden brown. Serve with salad of your choice.
Serves 6

Traditional noodle maker

Crispy Meatballs

✲ Kali Kebabs

1. Put the ground beef in a large bowl and set aside.

2. Soak the bread in water for about 2 minutes, then push the bread against a fine sieve to remove the water. Use the heel of your hard to squeeze all the water you can; this prevents the kebabs from falling apart when frying. Add the soaked and pressed bread to the ground beef.

3. Do the same thing with the grated onions and potatoes; push against a fine sieve to remove whatever moisture you can. Add to the ground beef.

4. In a separate bowl, combine the vegetable oil, garlic and ginger pastes, green chilies, salt, mint, cilantro and garam masala, mixing well. Add to the beef mixture.

5. Using your hands, knead the meat mixture thoroughly until it becomes very smooth.

6. Heat the oil in a large, deep skillet (or karahi) over medium-high heat.

7. Divide meat mixture into 15 portions and form each portion into a ball.

8. Add the meatballs and fry until almost dark brown. If you need to, work in batches. Drain on paper towels to absorb extra oil. Serve hot with lemon slices.

Makes 15 kebabs

Another Mogul classic, these beef kebabs are a specialty of Pakistan. Fragrant with mint leaves, they are a very popular Sunday brunch item in my house.

1 lb	500 g	ground beef
8–9	slices of bread
4 cups	1 L	water
2	medium onions, grated
2	medium potatoes, finely grated
3 Tbsp	45 mL	vegetable oil
1 Tbsp	15 mL	garlic paste (see page 177)
1 Tbsp	15 mL	ginger paste (see page 176)
1 Tbsp	15 mL	green chilies ground in a mortar and pestle
¾ tsp	4 mL	salt
2 Tbsp	30 mL	finely chopped mint
2 Tbsp	30 mL	finely chopped cilantro
1 tsp	5 mL	garam masala (see page 173)
4 cups	1 L	oil for deep-frying

Lamb Palak

Use tender cuts of lamb for this recipe and serve with plain white rice, Roti (page 144) and your chutney of choice.

1 lb | 500 g	lean lamb, cut into bite-sized pieces
1 cup | 250 mL	plain yogurt
1 Tbsp | 15 mL	garam masala (see page 173)
1 Tbsp | 15 mL	curry powder
½ cup | 125 mL	vegetable oil
2	large onions, sliced
½ cup | 125 mL	chopped cilantro
2 tsp | 10 mL	ginger paste (see page 176)
2 tsp | 10 mL	garlic paste (see page 177)
3	green chilies, chopped
3 bunches	spinach, blanched and finely chopped
	or
1	15 oz (425 g) can of spinach
2 cups | 500 mL	water
½ cup | 125 mL	whipping cream (35%)
½ tsp | 2 mL	salt
¼ cup | 60 mL	chopped cilantro

TEMPERING

3 Tbsp | 45 mL	vegetable oil
10–12	fenugreek seeds
½ tsp | 2 mL	cumin seeds
3 Tbsp | 45 mL	crispy fried onions (see page 57)

1. Combine the lamb, yogurt, garam masala and curry powder in a large glass bowl and mix well. Refrigerate for 3 hours.

2. Heat the oil in a large, deep skillet (or karahi) over medium-high heat. Fry the onions until almost brown.

3. Add the cilantro, ginger and garlic pastes and green chilies. Stir-fry for 3–4 minutes.

4. Add the lamb along with the marinade, reduce the heat to medium-low and cook for about 15 minutes.

5. If using fresh spinach, blanch and purée it and add it to the meat mixture. If using canned spinach, just add it to the meat mixture. Stir in the water. Cook for another 15 minutes, stirring occasionally.

6. When the lamb is almost done, increase the heat and cook, uncovered, until almost all the water is absorbed, about 10–12 minutes. Add the whipping cream and salt and bring to a boil. Remove from the heat and pour into a serving dish.

7. For the tempering, heat the oil in a small saucepan over high heat (see page 80). Add the fenugreek seeds and stir-fry for 30 seconds, then add the cumin seeds and immediately toss in the crispy fried onions. Pour the tempering mixture over the lamb palak. Garnish with the cilantro. Serve immediately. *Serves 4*

*Lamb Palak (facing page)
served with Roti (page 144)*

Lamb Korma

This traditional northern Indian dish has always been one of our family favorites. The word korma *simply denotes that it is a dish made with cream.*

1½ lb	750 g	lean boneless lamb
½ cup	125 mL	vegetable oil
½ cup	125 mL	crispy fried onions (see page 57)
1 tsp	5 mL	garam masala (see page 173)
1 Tbsp	15 mL	garlic paste (see page 177)
1 Tbsp	15 mL	ginger paste (see page 176)
2 Tbsp	30 mL	curry powder
1 tsp	5 mL	salt
1 cup	250 mL	plain yogurt
½ cup	125 mL	onion purée (see page 177)
½ cup	125 mL	water (if needed)
½ cup	125 mL	half-and-half cream

TEMPERING

3 Tbsp	45 mL	vegetable oil
22–26		fenugreek seeds
½ tsp	2 mL	cumin seeds
3 Tbsp	45 mL	crispy fried onions (see page 57)

GARNISH

½ cup	125 mL	slivered almonds
2		green chilies, finely chopped
½ cup	125 mL	chopped cilantro

1. Trim the meat and cut it into bite-sized pieces.

2. Heat the oil in a large, deep skillet (or karahi) over medium-high heat. Add the meat, crispy fried onions, garam masala, garlic and ginger pastes, curry powder, salt and yogurt. Stir well to coat the meat and cook for about 10 minutes until slightly browned.

3. Stir in the onion purée and cook for another 15 minutes. If the mixture is sticking to the pan, add some water, reduce the heat and simmer for another 10–12 minutes until the meat is tender.

4. Add the cream and bring to a boil, stirring occasionally. If the casserole is too dry, add up to another ½ cup (125 mL) of water. Remove from the heat and pour into a serving dish.

5. For the tempering, heat the oil in a small skillet over high heat. Add the fenugreek and cumin seeds and stir-fry for 30 seconds, then add the crispy fried onions.

6. Pour the tempering mixture over the casserole. Garnish with the slivered almonds, finely chopped green chilies and cilantro. Serve immediately. *Serves 6*

TAHERA'S TIPS

Tempering (also called waghai) is what we call the process of adding extra flavor to a dish directly before serving. It is a distinctly Indian cooking method that lends many dishes that special something. It involves heating a little oil and spices—often mustard seeds and curry leaves—over high heat for a minute or two and then drizzling over the dish. Try it and you'll taste the difference tempering can make.

Kashmiri Lamb Curry

1. Cut the meat into 2-inch (5 cm) cubes and set aside.

2. Combine the yogurt, almonds, garam masala, ginger and garlic pastes, salt, curry powder and red chili powder in a large bowl, mixing well. Add to the lamb and toss to coat.

3. Heat the oil in a large, deep skillet (or karahi) over medium-high heat. Add the crispy fried onions and cardamom and sauté for about 30 seconds.

4. Add the meat and yogurt mixture to the pan and cook for about 10 minutes, stirring occasionally.

5. Add 2 of the green chilies (keep one aside for garnish), the lemon juice and the tomatoes and cook for another 10 minutes.

6. Add the water, cover and simmer over low heat for about 25 minutes or until the meat is tender.

7. When the sauce has thickened, pour into a serving bowl and garnish with cilantro and the remaining chopped green chili. *Serves 8*

This national Kashmiri dish is now popular all over India. It's great for dinner parties when served with Naan (page 145).

2 lb | 1 kg	boneless lean lamb
½ cup | 125 mL	plain yogurt
¼ cup | 60 mL	slivered almonds
2 tsp | 10 mL	garam masala (see page 173)
2½ tsp | 12 mL	ginger paste (see page 176)
2½ tsp | 12 mL	garlic paste (see page 177)
¾ tsp | 4 mL	salt
1 tsp | 5 mL	curry powder
¾ tsp | 4 mL	red chili powder
½ cup | 125 mL	vegetable oil
½ cup | 125 mL	crispy fried onions (see page 57)
3	cardamom pods
3	green chilies, chopped
¼ cup | 60 mL	fresh lemon juice
1	19 oz (540 mL) can crushed tomatoes
1 cup | 250 mL	water
3 Tbsp | 45 mL	chopped cilantro

Rice with Fresh Lime (*Nimbu Chawal*) 86

Yogurt Rice (*Dahi Chawal*) 88

Lucknowi-Style Rice (*Khima Biryani*) 89

Pakistani-Style Rice (*Peshawari Biryani*) 90

Spiced Saffron Rice with Chicken (*Moghlai Murg Biryani*) 93

Royal Kedgeree (*Moghlai Khichdi*) 96

Casserole-Style Prawn Pilau 98

Zanzibari Pilau 99

Rice Dishes & Pilaus

Basmati rice, known for its aroma and nutty flavor, is very popular in Indian and Pakistani cuisine. It is the only rice that has that special fragrance and that can be served all by itself, spiced up as a pilaf, cooked with herbs such as dill, which is the Middle Eastern style, or baked with meats of your choice, which is the Mogul and Hyderabadi style.

I make it a point to tell all my students to look for the word "aged" on the bag before buying basmati rice. When it is aged, you will find that basmati has very few broken grains. The most popular brands are Punjab, Pakistani and Elephant brands from India. I like to use the Pakistani variety for its extra aroma and nutty flavor.

Other brands include Texmati, grown in Texas, and Kasmati, grown in Kansas. None of them have the strong aroma of the real basmati and they do not attain the long grain length. Calmati is brown basmati grown in California and I am still experimenting with it, trying it with dried fruits and nuts and different herbs.

Basmati rice is widely available and there is really no substitute when it comes to making delicious Indian rice dishes.

Although there are several ways of cooking basmati rice, make sure to always rinse basmati a couple of times and allow it to soak for 30 minutes in cold water before cooking.

METHOD ONE: SPAGHETTI STYLE

Cook the rice in a large pot of boiling water (spaghetti style). When the rice is almost done, about 15 minutes, drain in a fine colander, return to the pot and cover to finish the cooking process over low heat. Draining the water off gets rid of a lot of the starch.

METHOD TWO: TRADITIONAL STYLE

Cook rice at a ratio of 1¾ cups (425 mL) of water for the first 1 cup (250 mL) of rice, then 1½ cups (375 mL) of water for each additional 1 cup (250 mL) of rice. Bring to a boil, then cover and reduce the heat to low (keep the lid slightly open so it doesn't overboil). After the water is absorbed, about 10–12 minutes, continue cooking over low heat for 10 more minutes, uncovered.

METHOD THREE: BIRYANI STYLE

Bring a large ovenproof pot of water to a boil and add the rice. When the rice is almost done, about 15 minutes, drain off the water and cover. Place in a 250°F (120°C) oven for 30 minutes. I often use this method for biryani or other rich Mogul-style rice dishes.

STORING COOKED BASMATI

Cooked basmati can be refrigerated for up to 3 days. If you find that it is a bit dry by the third day, just sprinkle the rice with about ¼ cup (60 mL) of water, then either put it in the oven for about 30 minutes at 250°F (120°C) or microwave it on high power for 5–8 minutes. To freshen the flavor of leftover rice, pour 2 Tbsp (30 mL) of melted butter or vegetable oil over it.

Rice with Fresh Lime

※ *Nimbu Chawal*

The slightly tangy taste of this rice makes it an excellent accompaniment to any rich vegetable or prawn curry; I usually serve it with Chicken Karahi (page 56) or Lamb Palak (page 78).

2 cups ǀ 500 mL	basmati rice
3 cups ǀ 750 mL	water
¾ tsp ǀ 4 mL	sea salt
2	cardamom pods
3 Tbsp ǀ 45 mL	vegetable oil
1 tsp ǀ 5 mL	mustard seeds
2	shallots, chopped
6–7	curry leaves
2	green chilies, seeded and chopped
½ tsp ǀ 2 mL	black onion seeds
pinch	sea salt
¼ cup ǀ 60 mL	fresh lime juice

1. Rinse the rice and soak it in cold water for 30 minutes. Drain well.

2. Bring the 3 cups (750 mL) of water to a boil in a large saucepan over medium-high heat, then add the rice, the ¾ tsp (4 mL) of salt and the cardamom pods. Partially cover, reduce the heat to low and cook until the rice is almost tender and all the water has been absorbed, about 12–15 minutes.

3. Meanwhile, heat the oil in a large, deep skillet (or karahi) over medium-high heat. Add the mustard seeds and cook until they pop, about 20 seconds.

4. Add the chopped shallots, curry leaves, green chilies and black onion seeds. Sauté for about 2–3 minutes, then add the pinch of salt and lime juice. Cook for another minute or so.

5. Pour the spice mixture over the rice. Gently toss the rice with a fork and let sit for 10 minutes, covered, before serving. *Serves 4*

*Rice with Fresh Lime (facing page)
served alongside Lamb Korma (page 80)*

Yogurt Rice

* *Dahi Chawal*

Most Indian and Pakistani kitchens use yogurt, sometimes as a yogurt-based drink called lassi, sometimes as a thickening agent and marinade, and sometimes as a means to tone down spicy foods. This dish is an ideal accompaniment for spicy dishes, and the combination of yogurt and rice aids digestion. If you like, you can serve this with a garnish of chopped boiled eggs and thinly sliced red onions. Dahi simply means "yogurt" and chawal means "rice."

2 cups | 500 mL	basmati rice
3 cups | 750 mL	water
2	cardamom pods
¾ tsp | 4 mL	sea salt
3 Tbsp | 45 mL	vegetable oil
1 tsp | 5 mL	black mustard seeds
7	curry leaves
2	Kashmiri chilies (see page 61)
1½ Tbsp | 22 mL	chopped fresh ginger
½ tsp | 2 mL	black onion seeds
pinch	sea salt
1 cup | 250 mL	plain yogurt

1. Rinse and soak the rice for 30 minutes in cold water. Drain well.

2. Bring the 3 cups (750 mL) of water and the cardamom pods to a boil in a large saucepan. Add the rice and the ¾ tsp (4 mL) of salt. Partially cover, reduce the heat to low and continue to cook until the water is absorbed, about 12–15 minutes.

3. Meanwhile, heat the oil in a large frying pan over medium-high heat. When the oil is hot, add the mustard seeds. When they start to pop, add the curry leaves, chilies, ginger and black onion seeds. Sauté for about 1 minute. Add a pinch of salt and the yogurt, gently stirring all the time. Cook for another 2–3 minutes.

4. Pour the yogurt mixture over the rice and gently fluff it with a fork. Let stand for 5–10 minutes before serving.

Serves 4

Lucknowi-Style Rice

✳ Khima Biryani

1. Prepare the potatoes by peeling them and slicing them into ¼-inch (6 mm) discs. Heat 2 Tbsp (30 mL) of the oil in a large skillet over medium-high heat and fry the potato slices until tender inside and golden brown on the outside. Set aside.

2. Heat the remaining 2 Tbsp (30 mL) of oil in a large saucepan over medium-high heat, then add the ground beef, ginger and garlic pastes, salt, chili paste, curry powder and tomato paste.

3. Cook for at least 20 minutes or until all the liquid has evaporated. Add the water and saffron and cook for another 3 minutes.

4. Add the lemon juice and ¾ cup (185 mL) of the crispy fried onions. Cook for another 5 minutes. Remove from the heat and stir in the garam masala.

5. Preheat the oven to 120°F (50°C). Peel and slice the hard-boiled eggs.

6. Spread the meat mixture on the bottom of a 9- × 13-inch (3.5 L) casserole dish, then arrange all the egg slices over the meat. Add a layer of fried potatoes, then the corn, and finish off with a layer of the peas. Finally add the rice and decorate the top with the remaining crispy fried onions.

7. Heat through in the oven for about 20 minutes and serve. *Serves 6*

In the city of Lucknow in India this dish is often served as the finale to a festive meal. It can also be presented as a meal itself, accompanied by a salad and pickles. This recipe calls for ground beef, but chicken or mutton can also be used.

2	large potatoes
¼ cup | 60 mL	vegetable oil
2 lb | 1 kg	extra lean ground beef
1 tsp | 5 mL	ginger paste (see page 176)
1 tsp | 5 mL	garlic paste (see page 177)
½ tsp | 2 mL	salt
½ tsp | 2 mL	chili paste (sambal olek)
1 tsp | 5 mL	curry powder
2 tsp | 10 mL	tomato paste
1 cup | 250 mL	water
½ tsp | 2 mL	saffron threads
2 Tbsp | 30 mL	fresh lemon juice
1 cup | 250 mL	crispy fried onions (see page 57)
1 tsp | 5 mL	garam masala (see page 173)
4	hard-boiled eggs, cut crosswise into rings
2 cups | 500 mL	canned or frozen peaches and cream corn
2 cups | 500 mL	boiled peas
4 cups | 1 L	cooked basmati rice (see page 84)

Pakistani-Style Rice

❋ Peshawari Biryani

The rich, vibrant fragrance of the Indian spices in this impressive dish will warm your home. Splendid biryani, whether made with chicken, meat or fish, complements northern Indian and Pakistani celebration tables. The mixture is poured over the rice before serving.

MARINADE

2	green chilies
½ cup | 125 mL	chopped mint
1 tsp | 5 mL	ginger paste (see page 176)
1 tsp | 5 mL	garlic paste (see page 177)
1 cup | 250 mL	plain yogurt
4	boneless chicken breasts, cut into bite-sized pieces

(ingredients continued on page 92)

FOR THE MARINADE

1. Grind the chilies and mint in a food processor or mortar and pestle. In a small bowl, combine the chili and mint paste with the yogurt and the ginger and garlic pastes and stir to combine.

2. Pour the yogurt mixture over the chicken, ensuring the chicken is coated, and marinate the meat for at least 15–20 minutes in the refrigerator.

(continued on page 92)

Pakistani-Style Rice (facing page)
served with Onion Bread (page 155)

RICE

3½ cups | 840 mL	basmati rice
½ cup | 125 mL	vegetable oil
6	tomatoes, finely chopped
½ tsp | 2 mL	red chili powder
1½ tsp | 7 mL	roasted crushed coriander seeds
1 Tbsp | 15 mL	roasted crushed cumin seeds
1½ cups | 375 mL	crispy fried onions (see page 57)
1 cup | 250 mL	chopped green onions, chopped
1 cup | 250 mL	cooked (or canned) chickpeas
½ tsp | 2 mL	salt
3 cups | 750 mL	water
4	cardamom pods
1	cinnamon stick, in two 2-inch (5 cm) pieces
to taste	salt
½ tsp | 2 mL	saffron threads, soaked in 2 Tbsp (30 mL) hot water
3 Tbsp | 45 mL	fresh lemon juice
½ cup | 125 mL	chopped sweet onion
½ cup | 125 mL	chopped cilantro

FOR THE RICE

1. Meanwhile, rinse the rice and soak it for 20–30 minutes in cold water. Drain well.

2. Heat the oil in a large, deep skillet (or karahi) over medium heat. Add the tomatoes and red chili powder and sauté for about 10 minutes.

3. Stir in the marinated chicken and then add the roasted coriander and cumin seeds. Cook for 10–12 minutes, or until the meat is almost cooked through. Add 1 cup (250 mL) of the crispy fried onions, then add the green onions, chickpeas and salt and mix well. Continue to cook over low heat.

4. While the chicken is cooking, bring the 3 cups (750 mL) of water to a boil in a large saucepan. Simmer for 1–2 minutes with the cardamom, cinnamon sticks and salt. Add the rice and cook until tender, approximately 10 minutes.

5. Drain the rice well in a fine sieve and place on a large serving platter. Sprinkle with the saffron water, lemon juice and the remaining ½ cup (125 mL) of crispy fried onions.

6. Pour the meat mixture over the rice and garnish with the chopped sweet onion and cilantro. Serve with a plate of sliced cucumber or pickle of your choice. *Serves 6*

Spiced Saffron Rice with Chicken

❋ Moghlai Murg Biryani

FOR THE MARINADE

1. For the marinade, combine the ginger and garlic pastes, lemon juice, salt, chili paste, yogurt, cardamom and nutmeg in a glass bowl. Add the chicken and mix well. Marinate in the refrigerator for 1 hour.

(continued on page 95)

This is a festive dish and in India it is usually served on the Idd days after the fasting month of Ramadhan. There are numerous versions of this dish but this is the one I make at home for my family or when I have a large gathering.

MARINADE

1 tsp	5 mL	ginger paste (see page 176)
1 tsp	5 mL	garlic paste (see page 177)
¼ cup	60 mL	fresh lemon juice
½ tsp	2 mL	salt
¼ tsp	1 mL	chili paste (sambal olek)
1 cup	250 mL	plain yogurt
¼ tsp	1 mL	ground cardamom
¼ tsp	1 mL	ground nutmeg
1 lb	500 g	boneless chicken breast, cut into bite-sized pieces

(ingredients continued on page 95)

FOR THE RICE

1. Meanwhile, rinse the rice and soak it for 30 minutes in cold water. Drain well.

2. Combine the 12 cups (3 L) water with the salt, cardamom pods and cinnamon stick and bring to a boil. Add the rice and cook until tender, about 10–12 minutes. Remove the rice from the heat and drain in a large sieve.

3. Mix the cashews, pistachios, almonds and ginger strips in a large bowl.

4. Place a layer of the cooked rice in a 9- × 13-inch (3.5 L) casserole dish and sprinkle with a layer of the nut mixture. Continue the layers until all the rice and nuts are used.

5. Mix the saffron, water and yellow food coloring and sprinkle over the rice; cover tightly with a lid or plastic wrap and set aside.

6. Heat the oil in a large, deep skillet (or karahi) over medium-high heat and add chicken and marinade. Cook for at least 15–20 minutes until the meat is cooked through. The mixture should be thick and not runny.

7. Stir the crispy fried onions into the meat. This will absorb any excess liquid and form nice thick gravy. Transfer the rice to a large platter and pour the meat mixture over the rice. Serve immediately. *Serves 6*

RICE

4 cups | 1 L	basmati rice
12 cups | 3 L	water
2 tsp | 10 mL	salt
2	cardamom pods
½	cinnamon stick (2 inches/5 cm)
½ cup | 125 mL	unsalted cashew nuts
½ cup | 125 mL	pistachios
½ cup | 125 mL	slivered almonds
1 piece	ginger (3 inches/8 cm), peeled and cut into thin strips
¼ tsp | 1 mL	saffron threads
¼ cup | 1 mL	boiling water
¼ tsp | 1 mL	yellow food coloring (optional)
½ cup | 125 mL	vegetable oil
2½ cups | 625 mL	crispy fried onions (see page 57)

Royal Kedgeree

❋ *Moghlai Khichdi*

In India and Pakistan yogurt is commonly used as a cooling refresher to offset the fiery spices. The richness of the butter, crispy fried onions, cardamom and yogurt makes this dish irresistible.

MEAT MIXTURE

3 Tbsp | 45 mL	butter
¾ lb | 340 g	extra lean ground beef
1 tsp | 5 mL	salt
1½ cups | 375 mL	plain yogurt
1 tsp | 5 mL	ginger paste (see page 176)
1 tsp | 5 mL	garlic paste (see page 177)
½ cup | 125 mL	finely crushed crispy fried onions (see page 57)
1	green chili, chopped
¼ cup | 60 mL	chopped mint
1 tsp | 5 mL	curry powder
½ tsp | 2 mL	ground cardamom
½ tsp | 2 mL	garam masala (see page 173)

FOR THE MEAT MIXTURE

1. Heat the butter in a medium-sized skillet or saucepan over medium-high heat, add the ground beef and sauté until the meat is no longer pink.

2. Add the salt, yogurt, ginger and garlic pastes and crushed crispy fried onions. Stir well and sauté for another 10–12 minutes.

3. Add the chili, mint, curry powder, cardamom and garam masala. Continue cooking until all the liquid is absorbed. Set aside.

FOR THE RICE

1. Meanwhile, rinse the rice and soak it for 30 minutes in cold water. Drain well.

2. Melt the butter in a large saucepan on medium-high heat and sauté the slivered onion until light golden brown. Stir in the garlic paste, chopped ginger, peppercorns, cinnamon stick, cardamom and cumin seeds and sauté for 1 minute.

3. Add the milk, water and salt and bring to boil.

4. Add the soaked and drained rice, mung daal and crispy fried onions. Stir well before partially covering the pot. Cook on low heat until the rice and daal are tender, about 15 minutes.

5. Stir the meat mixture into the rice and simmer over low heat for at least 20 minutes before serving. Garnish with the chopped cilantro and serve with lemon or mango pickles. *Serves 4*

RICE

1½ cups | 375 mL	basmati rice
¼ cup | 60 mL	butter
1	medium red onion, slivered
1 tsp | 5 mL	garlic paste (see page 177)
1 piece	ginger (1 inch/2.5 cm), finely chopped
6	black peppercorns
¼	cinnamon stick (1 inch/2.5 cm)
3	cardamom pods
1 tsp | 5 mL	roasted cumin seeds
1½ cups | 375 mL	milk
2 cups | 500 mL	water
¾ tsp | 4 mL	salt
½ cup | 125 mL	mung daal
½ cup | 125 mL	crispy fried onions (see page 57)
½ cup | 125 mL	chopped cilantro

Casserole-Style Prawn Pilau

There are plenty of seafood delights in the crowded corridors of Indian cuisine, especially those from Goa, on the west coast of India, which is known for its excellent seafood dishes. This dish should be moist and the prawns tender. Serve it with salad and Red Coconut Chutney (page 163).

3 cups | 750 mL	basmati rice
1 lb | 500 g	raw tiger prawns
1 bunch	cilantro, chopped
3 Tbsp | 45 mL	grated fresh coconut
1 bunch	green onions, chopped
1	green chilies, finely chopped
1 tsp | 5 mL	salt
3 Tbsp | 45 mL	vegetable oil
1 tsp | 5 mL	curry powder
½ tsp | 2 mL	ground turmeric
4	large tomatoes, finely chopped
3	eggs
to taste	salt and pepper
1 Tbsp | 15 mL	butter

1. Rinse and soak the rice in cold water for 20–30 minutes. Drain.

2. Meanwhile, peel and devein the prawns. Set aside. Combine half of the cilantro, coconut, green onions and green chilies in a bowl and set aside.

3. Bring a large pot of water to a boil with the salt and cook the rice spaghetti style (see page 85). When the rice is done, about 12 minutes, drain well in a colander.

4. Preheat the oven to 400°F (200°C).

5. Heat the oil in a large, deep skillet (or karahi) over medium-high heat. Add the curry powder, turmeric and tomatoes. Stir and cook for 1 minute, then add the prawns and the cilantro, coconut, green onion and green chili mixture. Cook for 3–5 minutes, until prawns are pink and the mixture is heated through.

6. Beat the eggs in a small bowl and add any extra tomato juice and spice from the saucepan. Season with salt and pepper and mix well.

7. Transfer the rice to a large ovenproof casserole dish and spread the prawn mixture overtop. Pour the egg mixture over the prawns and dot small lumps of butter here and there. Bake for 10–15 minutes.

8. Garnish with the remaining cilantro and serve immediately. *Serves 4–6*

Zanzibari Pilau

1. Cut the meat into bite-sized pieces. Place the veal in a large saucepan with the water and bring to a boil.

2. Add 1 tsp (5 mL) of the garlic paste, the ginger paste and 1 stick of cinnamon. Continue cooking on medium-high for about 20 minutes, until the meat is cooked through. Set aside.

3. Heat the oil in a large, deep skillet (or karahi) over medium-high heat. Add the onion and sauté for 3 minutes, then add the tomato and cook for an additional 2 minutes, stirring constantly to make sure it does not stick to the pan.

4. Add the remaining 1 tsp (5 mL) garlic paste, the remaining 2 cinnamon sticks, cumin seeds, peppercorns, cloves, green chilies and cardamom pods. Cook for 4–5 minutes. Add the potatoes and cook for 5 minutes. Stir in the yogurt, coconut milk and salt and bring to a boil.

5. Add the cooked meat to the mixture, along with 1½ cups (375 mL) of the meat broth. If there is not enough broth, top it off with enough water to make 1½ cups (375 mL). Continue cooking over medium-high heat.

6. Rinse and soak the rice for 20–30 minutes in enough cold water to cover.

7. When the potatoes are almost done, add the drained rice. Cook until all the liquid is absorbed and the mixture is dry. If the rice is not quite cooked, sprinkle with 1–2 Tbsp (15–30 mL) of water, cover with a lid and place in a 300°F (150°C) oven for about 15 minutes. *Serves 4–6*

This dish is a specialty in Zanzibar— where I come from—an island off Tanzania on the east coast of Africa. Every Saturday most of the islanders serve this for lunch with their famous coconut chutney. This pilau can also be used as an accompaniment to curries and pickles.

1 lb | 500 g	veal, with bones
2 cups | 500 mL	water
2 tsp | 10 mL	garlic paste (see page 177)
1 tsp | 5 mL	ginger paste (see page 176)
1	cinnamon stick, in three 1-inch (2.5 cm) pieces
5 Tbsp | 75 mL	vegetable oil
1	medium onion, chopped
1	medium tomato, chopped
1 Tbsp | 15 mL	roasted cumin seeds
9–10	black peppercorns
3	whole cloves
2	green chilies, chopped
4	cardamom pods
2	large potatoes, peeled and cut into bite-sized chunks
1 cup | 250 mL	plain yogurt
1	14 oz (398 mL) can coconut milk
1 tsp | 5 mL	sea salt
3 cups | 750 mL	basmati rice

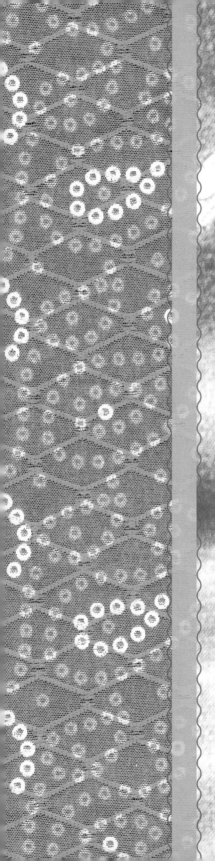

Spinach & Lentil Daal (*Palak Masoor Daal*) 102

Rajastani Daal 103

Sudanese-Style Fava Beans (*Foul Medammas*) 104

Lentil & Flat Bean Curry (*Bhendi Guvar Daal*) 106

Red Kidney Bean Curry (*Rajma Kadhi*) 108

Royal Curry (*Shahi Kadhi*) 109

Pigeon Peas in Coconut Sauce (*Barazi*) 110

Cauliflower with Potatoes (*Alu Gobi Masala*) 111

Potato & Egg Curry (*Alu Baida Kadhi*) 112

Cauliflower & Pea Curry (*Matar Gobi Masala*) 113

Squash Kofta Curry (*Dudhi Kadhi Kofta*) 114

Green Peas in Coconut Curry (*Naryal Matar Kadhi*) 117

Pea & Fenugreek Curry (*Matar Methi Malai*) 118

Almond & Vegetable Curry (*Sabji Badam Kadhi*) 119

Vegetarian Curries

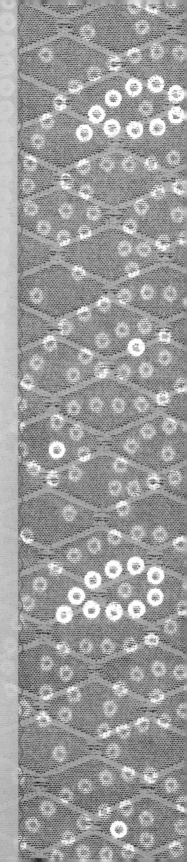

Spinach & Lentil Daal

✴ Palak Masoor Daal

Daals are not usually associated with spinach (palak), so this dish may surprise you. Not only does it taste good, but it looks good too. Those who love spices can add a couple of green chilies to give it that special kick. This dish will warm you up from the inside out, which makes it particularly good on a cold winter's day. It's best if you have a pressure cooker, since it makes this recipe quicker to prepare. Serve it with rice.

1 cup | 250 mL	masoor daal
1 bunch	spinach
1	onion
1	tomato
3	green chilies
1 tsp | 5 mL	garlic paste (see page 177)
1 tsp | 5 mL	ginger paste (see page 176)
3 Tbsp | 45 mL	oil
½ tsp | 2 mL	cumin seeds
1 Tbsp | 15 mL	dried fenugreek leaves
1½ tsp | 7 mL	turmeric
¼ tsp | 1 mL	red chili powder
½ tsp | 2 mL	dried mango powder
to taste	salt

1. Rinse the daal. If using a pressure cooker, place the daal and ½ cup (125 mL) of water in a pressure cooker on medium heat. If using the stovetop, cover the daal with water and bring to a boil. Reduce the heat to medium-low and cook for 40 minutes.

2. Wash and chop the spinach and set it aside. Finely chop the onion and tomato and set aside.

3. Using a food processor, or a mortar and pestle, grind the green chilies to a fine paste. Combine this chili paste with the garlic and ginger pastes and set aside.

4. Heat the oil in a large, deep skillet (or karahi) over medium-high heat.

5. Add the cumin seeds, then add the reserved onion and sauté until it is golden brown, about 4 minutes. Stir in the fenugreek leaves and sauté for about 30 seconds. Add the ginger, garlic and chili paste mixture, the turmeric, red chili powder, mango powder and reserved tomato.

6. Add the daal, spinach and salt. Cook over medium heat for about 10 minutes. Serve hot. *Serves 4*

Rajastani Daal

1. Soak the urad daal and kidney beans (if using dried kidney beans) in cold water overnight. If using canned kidney beans, simply drain and rinse them under plenty of cold water. Drain well.

2. Place the urad daal, kidney beans, onion, ginger and garlic pastes, turmeric, red chili powder, garam masala and water in a pressure cooker. Cook over medium-high heat for about 10–12 minutes. If you don't have a pressure cooker, combine all the ingredients in a large saucepan. Bring to a boil, then reduce to a simmer, adding water as needed for about 45 minutes.

3. Place the ghee in a large, deep skillet (or karahi) over medium heat and add the tomato paste. Add the cooked daal and bean mixture and the green chilies. Simmer until well mixed until heated through.

4. Stir in the cream and the cilantro and serve immediately. *Serves 4*

This dish hails from its namesake: Rajastan state in India. Serve this with Zanibari Pilau (page 99) or any Indian bread and pickle.

½ cup | 125 mL	urad daal
1 cup | 250 mL	dried kidney beans
	or
1	14 oz (398 mL) can kidney beans
2	onions, chopped
1 tsp | 5 mL	ginger paste (see page 176)
1 tsp | 5 mL	garlic paste (see page 177)
½ tsp | 2 mL	turmeric
½ tsp | 2 mL	red chili powder
½ tsp | 2 mL	garam masala (see page 173)
8 cups | 2 L	water
½ cup | 125 mL	ghee (clarified butter)
1 Tbsp | 15 mL	tomato paste
4	green chilies, chopped
½ cup | 125 mL	half-and-half cream
½ cup | 125 mL	chopped cilantro

Sudanese-Style Fava Beans

❊ Foul Medammas

Foul (pronounced "fool") is one of many names for the fava bean. My family looks forward to this simple and delicious dish once a week. I learned how to make it when I was living in Zaire, very close to the Sudanese border. Pita bread or Roti (page 144) is a good accompaniment to this meal.

2 cups | 500 mL	dry fava beans
	or
2	14 oz (398 mL) cans fava beans
½ cup | 125 mL	olive oil
½ cup | 125 mL	chopped mint
1 Tbsp | 15 mL	garlic paste (see page 177)
1	large white onion, chopped
2 Tbsp | 30 mL	fresh lemon juice
½ tsp | 2 mL	ground black pepper
to taste	sea salt
1	tomato, finely chopped
2 Tbsp | 30 mL	chopped cilantro

1. If you are using dry fava beans, soak them overnight. Drain and bring them to a boil with plenty of fresh water in a medium saucepan over medium-high heat. Cook until tender, approximately 45 minutes, then drain. If you are using canned beans, simply rinse them under cold water and put in a large saucepan with plenty of fresh water. Bring to a boil until the beans are heated through and drain. Return to the saucepan, reserving 3 Tbsp (45 mL) of the beans.

2. Purée the reserved beans in a food processor and return to the saucepan with the whole beans.

3. Add the olive oil, mint, garlic paste, onion, lemon juice, pepper and salt. Reduce heat to low for about 10 minutes. Mix well just once.

4. Pour into a serving bowl and garnish with the chopped tomatoes and cilantro. *Serves 4*

Lentil & Flat Bean Curry

* Bhendi Guvar Daal

This is a cross between a lentil and fresh vegetable curry and is usually served as part of a thali meal in restaurants in India. Thali is a platter with 3–4 different types of curry served with, a chapati and rice. Serve this curry with Roti (page 144) or over a bed of rice.

1 cup | 250 mL	yellow mung daal
2 oz | 60 g	guvar beans
4 cups | 1 L	water
¼ tsp | 1 mL	turmeric
to taste	salt
2	medium tomatoes, chopped
4–5	curry leaves
5	green chilies, chopped
1 piece	ginger (1 inch/2.5 cm)
¼ lb | 125 g	okra (fresh or frozen)
3 Tbsp | 45 mL	oil
¼ tsp | 1 mL	asafetida (see page 22)
1 tsp | 5 mL	cumin seeds
1 tsp | 5 mL	red chili powder
4–5	kokam leaves, torn into pieces

1. Soak the yellow mung daal for 30 minutes in cold water and drain.

2. Prepare the guvar beans by trimming both ends but leaving them whole.

3. In a medium-sized saucepan, combine the water, daal, turmeric and salt. Bring to a boil.

4. Reduce and simmer until the daal is tender, about 12–15 minutes. Stir well and add the guvar beans, tomatoes, curry leaves, chopped green chilies, ginger and okra. Make sure there is enough water to just cover the vegetables. Cover and cook over medium heat until tender, about 10 minutes.

5. Meanwhile, heat the oil in a small saucepan over medium heat. Add the asafetida, cumin seeds and the red chili powder. Stir-fry for about 20 seconds and drizzle over the tomato and bean mixture.

6. Finally add the kokam leaves and serve. *Serves 4*

TAHERA'S TIPS

Guvar beans are fresh, flat green beans that are also known as cluster beans. Kokam leaves are a specialty Indian spice and you can find them in any Indian grocery store.

Spiced Bean & Cucumber Salad
(page 41)

Drumsticks with Potatoes (page 133)

Lentil & Flat Bean Curry (facing page)

Red Kidney Bean Curry

✳ Rajma Kadhi

*This is another favorite of my son Zuber.
It is rich, nutritious and full of protein.
Canned red kidney beans can be used
if you are in a hurry, but I like to use
the dried ones, as I find they are tastier
and the texture is better. Serve with rice,
Paratha (page 145) or Naan (page 143).*

2 cups | 500 mL	dry kidney beans
	or
2	14 oz (398 mL) cans
	kidney beans
3 Tbsp | 45 mL	oil
1 cup | 250 mL	chopped onion
3	bay leaves
1½ Tbsp | 22 mL	ginger paste (see page 176)
1 Tbsp | 15 mL	garlic paste (see page 177)
1 tsp | 5 mL	garam masala
	(see page 173)
1 Tbsp | 15 mL	red chili powder
1 Tbsp | 15 mL	ground coriander
1 tsp | 5 mL	turmeric
1 tsp | 5 mL	ground cumin
1½ cups | 375 mL	chopped tomato
½ cup | 125 mL	milk
½ cup | 125 mL	water, as needed
to taste	salt
¼ cup | 60 mL	chopped cilantro
2 Tbsp | 30 mL	fresh lemon juice

1. Rinse and soak the kidney beans overnight in enough cold water to cover them. Drain and set aside. If using canned beans, rinse and set aside.

2. Combine the kidney beans and water in a large saucepan. Cover partially and bring to a boil over medium-high heat. Cook for about 15 minutes or until the beans are tender.

3. Heat the oil in another saucepan on medium-high heat, add the onion and bay leaves and sauté until they are golden brown, about 7–10 minutes. Add the ginger and garlic pastes and continue to sauté for about 30 seconds.

4. Stir in the garam masala, red chili powder, ground coriander, turmeric, cumin and the chopped tomato. Cook for another 30–40 seconds or until heated through.

5. Add the milk and the cooked beans, stirring well so the beans are all well coated with the gravy. Bring to a simmer for 5 minutes. If you find there is too little gravy, add the water. The amount of gravy required depends on whether you're serving it with rice or naan.

6. Stir in the salt and half of the chopped cilantro. Pour into a serving dish and sprinkle with the fresh lemon juice and the remaining cilantro. *Serves 4*

Royal Curry

❋ Shahi Kadhi

1. If using dried beans, soak the beans overnight in cold water. Drain and set aside. If using canned beans, rinse and set aside.

2. Combine the chopped tomatoes and 1½ cups (375 mL) of water in a saucepan over medium-high heat and cook until the tomatoes are soft, about 8–10 minutes. Pass the tomatoes through a sieve to make a purée, or purée in a food processor. Set aside.

3. Place the onion, poppy seeds, green chilies, coriander seeds, aniseed, cardamom pods, cumin seeds, ginger, cloves and cinnamon in the bowl of a food processor. Grind to a paste. If you need to, add a bit of water so it forms a thick paste.

4. Heat the oil in a medium-sized skillet or saucepan over medium-high heat and sauté the spice paste for 2–3 minutes until it's light brown and fragrant.

5. Add the tomato purée, sugar, kidney beans, carrots and cauliflower and cook until the vegetables are tender, about 10 minutes.

6. Add the salt and serve hot. *Serves 4*

Most Indians are vegetarians, and the kidney beans in this curry are a great way of providing necessary protein in the diet. Serve this at brunch or as part of a main meal. This dish is perfect when served with potatoes and sliced sweet onions on the side.

½ cup | 125 mL	dry kidney beans
	or
1	14 oz (398 mL) can kidney beans
3	large tomatoes, chopped
1½ cups | 375 mL	water
1	large onion, chopped
1 Tbsp | 15 mL	poppy seeds
2	green chilies
1 Tbsp | 15 mL	coriander seeds
2 tsp | 10 mL	aniseed
3	cardamom pods
1 Tbsp | 15 mL	cumin seeds
1 piece	ginger (½ inch/1 cm), chopped
3	cloves
½	cinnamon stick (2 inches/5 cm)
1 Tbsp | 15 mL	oil
½ tsp | 2 mL	sugar
2	carrots, chopped
12–15	large cauliflower florets
to taste	salt

Pigeon Peas in Coconut Sauce

❈ Barazi

This is a very common dish among East Indian families living on the island of Zanzibar. It is usually served with Mandazi, which I call African Donuts (page 150), during the month of Ramadhan, but we also have it for breakfast on Sundays. Turn this into a complete meal by serving it with plain basmati rice, Roti (page 144) and a salad.

3 cups | 750 mL	dried pigeon peas (toor daal)
	or
3	14 oz (398 mL) cans pigeon peas
2	medium tomatoes, chopped
1	medium onion, chopped
4	green chilies, sliced in half
½ tsp | 2 mL	turmeric
2½ cups | 625 mL	coconut milk
¾ tsp | 7 mL	salt

1. If using dried beans, place the dried pigeon peas in a large bowl and add enough water to cover. Soak overnight and drain. If using canned pigeon peas, simply rinse with cold water.

2. Place the peas in a large saucepan. Cover with plenty of fresh water (enough to come at least 3 inches/7.5 cm above the peas). Cook over medium-high heat until tender, about 30 minutes.

3. Drain and return to the saucepan over medium heat. Add the tomatoes, onion, green chilies, turmeric, coconut milk and salt and stir.

4. Bring to a boil and cook for another 5 minutes.

5. Turn the heat off and set the saucepan aside for 10–15 minutes. Before serving, heat through. *Serves 6*

TAHERA'S TIPS

Pigeon peas (also known as toor daal) can be found dried, canned and even frozen in Indian grocery stores and even in several Western grocery stores. I prefer the dried ones (pictured on page 5). This dish can be made in advance and frozen for 2–3 weeks.

Cauliflower with Potatoes

❊ *Alu Gobi Masala*

1. Prepare the cauliflower by bringing the water, salt and turmeric to a boil in a large saucepan. Turn off the heat. Add the cauliflower to the water. Cover the pan and set aside for 3 minutes. Drain the water and rinse the cauliflower well. Set aside.

2. Prepare the potatoes by washing them and placing them in a large saucepan of water over high heat. Boil them until tender, about 8–10 minutes. Allow them to cool. Peel and cut each potato into 4 or 6 pieces. Set aside.

3. Heat the oil in a large, deep skillet (or karahi) over medium-high heat and add the mustard seeds. When they start to pop, add the urad daal and fry until golden.

4. Reduce the heat to medium, add the garlic and ginger pastes and fry for 30 seconds. Add the onion and fry until translucent, about 1–2 minutes. Add the chopped tomato and sauté for about 3 minutes.

5. Add the crushed tomatoes, reserved cauliflower and potatoes and cook for 3–4 minutes.

6. Add the red chili powder, turmeric and salt. Mix well and sprinkle with the water so it doesn't stick to the pan. Turn the heat to low and simmer for 10 minutes. Sprinkle with cilantro and serve immediately. *Serves 4–6*

TAHERA'S TIPS
I find it is easier to peel and cut potatoes after they are cooked. They tend to keep their shape better.

This dainty vegetarian dish truly enhances a meatless meal, and it will find favor among nonvegetarians too. Although it's a specialty of the Punjab region, it is cooked universally. Serve it with rice, Naan (page 143) or Paratha (page 145).

2 cups | 500 mL	water
½ tsp | 2 mL	salt
¼ tsp | 1 mL	turmeric
1	medium cauliflower, cut into florets
4	medium potatoes
¼ cup | 60 mL	vegetable oil
1 tsp | 5 mL	mustard seeds
½ tsp | 2 mL	dry urad daal
1 tsp | 5 mL	garlic paste (see page 177)
1 tsp | 5 mL	ginger paste (see page 176)
1	medium onion, chopped
1	medium tomato, chopped
¼ cup | 60 mL	crushed tomatoes
1 tsp | 5 mL	red chili powder
¼ tsp | 1 mL	turmeric
to taste	salt
½ cup | 125 mL	water
½ cup | 125 mL	chopped cilantro

Potato & Egg Curry

❊ Alu Baida Kadhi

Quick, easy and perfect with Puri (page 147) or Roti (page 144), this curry is great for a light dinner.

5–6	medium potatoes
4	large onions
5 Tbsp ∣ 75 mL	vegetable oil
1	green chili, finely chopped (optional)
½ tsp ∣ 2 mL	garlic paste (see page 177)
½ tsp ∣ 2 mL	turmeric
½ tsp ∣ 2 mL	cumin seeds
to taste	salt
4	eggs, beaten
½ cup ∣ 125 mL	water, as needed
2 Tbsp ∣ 30 mL	chopped cilantro

1. Peel the potatoes and cut into bite-sized pieces; set aside. Slice the onion into thin rings and set aside.

2. Heat the oil in a large, deep skillet (or karahi) on medium-high. Add the potatoes and sauté for about 10 minutes.

3. Add the onions and sauté for another 8–10 minutes.

4. Add the chopped green chili, garlic paste, turmeric, cumin seeds and salt. Cook for about 2 minutes.

5. Add the beaten egg and mix until the onions and potatoes are coated with egg and well cooked. Note that if the curry is very thick, add just enough water to bring it to a consistency that can be mixed but is still thick. (The onions often provide enough moisture but this varies with the type of onion.)

6. Place on a serving dish and garnish with cilantro.
   Serves 4–6

Cauliflower & Pea Curry

✳ *Matar Gobi Masala*

1. Separate the cauliflower into large florets. Soak in cold water for 10 minutes and drain. Set aside.

2. Put the peas in a medium-sized saucepan with 2 cups (500 mL) of water over high heat. Cook the peas with a pinch of baking soda and salt for about 8–10 minutes. Drain and set aside.

3. Heat the oil in a large, deep skillet (or karahi) and add the mustard seeds. When the mustard seeds begin to pop, add the green chilies and cook for 30 seconds.

4. Add the cauliflower florets and salt to taste. Sauté for 1–2 minutes. Lower the heat to medium-low, cover and continue to cook for 10 minutes, stirring frequently.

5. When the cauliflower is almost tender, add the peas.

6. In a small bowl, combine the cumin, turmeric, ground coriander and red chili powder. Add to the cauliflower. Stir and cook over high heat for 3 minutes.

7. Garnish with cilantro and serve immediately. *Serves 4–6*

This dish is a favorite all over India, and, when I teach it in my vegetarian cooking classes, it is a favorite with Canadians as well. Serve it with Paratha (page 145) or Naan (page 143).

1	medium cauliflower
1 cup | 250 mL	frozen green peas
pinch	baking soda
pinch	salt
3 Tbsp | 45 mL	vegetable oil
½ tsp | 2 mL	mustard seeds
3	green chilies, chopped
to taste	salt
½ tsp | 2 mL	cumin
½ tsp | 2 mL	turmeric
½ tsp | 2 mL	ground coriander
½ tsp | 2 mL	red chili powder
¼ cup | 60 mL	chopped cilantro

Squash Kofta Curry

❋ *Dudhi Kadhi Kofta*

This is a moist dish that goes well with rice or any Indian-style bread. We call it kofta, which just means any spice mixture that is formed into small balls and cooked. Dudhi is simply the Hindi word for the vegetable that is referred to as "bottle gourd" or "calabash" in English.

KOFTA

1 lb | 500 g	dudhi (or bottle gourd)
¼ cup | 60 mL	finely chopped cilantro
3	green chilies, finely chopped
2 tsp | 10 mL	ground coriander
4 Tbsp | 60 mL	chana flour (see page 18)
½ tsp | 2 mL	coarsely ground cumin
1½ tsp | 7 mL	red chili powder
pinch	turmeric
to taste	salt
2 cups | 500 mL	oil for deep-frying

FOR THE KOFTAS

1. Grate the dudhi and squeeze out all the water by pressing it against a fine sieve using the heel of your hand.

2. In a small bowl, combine the cilantro, green chilies, coriander, chana flour, cumin, red chili powder, turmeric and salt. Add to the grated dudhi and mix well.

3. Heat the oil in a large, deep skillet (or karahi) over medium-high heat. Form the mixture into 2-inch (5 cm) balls and, when the oil is hot, fry the balls until they are golden brown, about 3 minutes. Remove from the oil and set aside on a plate covered with paper towels.

FOR THE GRAVY

1. Finely grate the onions and squeeze out all the water by pressing the onion against a fine sieve using the heel of your hand.

2. Heat the oil in a large, deep skillet (or karahi) over medium-high heat. Add the grated onions, green chilies, ginger and garlic pastes, turmeric, cumin seeds, cardamom, cloves, red chili powder and coriander. Sauté until golden brown.

3. Add the chopped tomatoes and salt to taste. Continue cooking over medium heat for about 3 or 4 minutes.

4. Stir in the 1 cup (250 mL) of water to make a gravy and mix well. Add the koftas to the gravy and cook over medium heat until the curry and the koftas are heated through. Garnish with coriander leaves and serve. *Serves 4–6*

TAHERA'S TIPS
If you have trouble finding a dudhi, try using any kind of squash as a substitute.

GRAVY

2	medium onions
5 Tbsp | 75 mL	oil
3	green chilies, finely chopped
1 tsp | 5 mL	ginger paste (see page 176)
1 tsp | 5 mL	garlic paste (see page 177)
¼ tsp | 1 mL	turmeric
½ tsp | 2 mL	cumin seeds
1	black cardamom pod
2	whole cloves
2 tsp | 10 mL	red chili powder
2 tsp | 10 mL	ground coriander
2	medium tomatoes, finely chopped
to taste	salt
1 cup | 250 mL	water
¼ cup | 60 mL	chopped cilantro

Green Peas in Coconut Curry

☀ Naryal Matar Kadhi

1. Place the peas in a microwave-safe dish and microwave on high for 4 minutes. Set aside.

2. Heat the vegetable oil in a saucepan over medium-high heat. Add the mustard seeds and curry leaves and sauté until the mustard seeds start to pop, about 30 seconds.

3. Stir in the chopped onions and fry for about 3–4 minutes, or until it produces a nice fragrance.

4. Add the garlic paste, turmeric, red chili powder and tomatoes. Reduce the heat to low and cook for about 3–4 minutes.

5. Add the peas, salt, coconut milk and lemon juice. Stir gently and bring to a boil.

6. Switch off the heat and let sit for 30 minutes to thicken slightly.

7. Pour into a serving bowl and garnish with the cilantro.

Serves 4–6

I learned to cook this dish, which is very popular in Gujarat state, from my mother's friend Kussum. Peas are a favorite in my family, and because my husband really likes them, I tend to cook this dish quite often. Serve this with Paratha (page 145) or plain rice.

4 cups | 1 L	frozen peas
¼ cup | 60 mL	vegetable oil
½ tsp | 2 mL	black mustard seeds
4	curry leaves
2	medium onions, finely chopped
½ tsp | 2 mL	garlic paste (see page 177)
½ tsp | 2 mL	turmeric
½ tsp | 2 mL	red chili powder
2	medium tomatoes, finely chopped
to taste	salt
1	14 oz (398 mL) can coconut milk
2 Tbsp | 30 mL	fresh lemon juice
3 Tbsp | 45 mL	chopped cilantro

Pea & Fenugreek Curry

❉ *Matar Methi Malai*

Feel free to experiment with adding different vegetables to this delicious dish. Instead of using peas, try using canned peaches and cream corn. You could also try adding cinnamon instead of the garam masala.

2 cups	500 mL	fresh fenugreek leaves
1 tsp	2 mL	salt
1½ Tbsp	22 mL	oil
½ cup	125 mL	chopped onion
2 Tbsp	30 mL	ginger paste (see page 176)
2 Tbsp	30 mL	garlic paste (see page 177)
1 tsp	5 mL	red chili powder
1 cup	250 mL	frozen green peas
½ tsp	2 mL	dried mango powder
½ cup	125 mL	whipping cream (35%)
¼ tsp	1 mL	garam masala (see page 173)
to taste		salt

1. Rinse the fenugreek leaves, put them in a bowl and sprinkle ½ tsp (2 mL) of salt over them. Let them sit for 10 minutes. Then wash them again to remove the excess salt. Set aside.

2. Heat the oil in a large, deep skillet (or karahi) over medium-high heat. Add the onion and sauté for about 4–5 minutes.

3. Stir in the ginger and garlic pastes and the reserved fenugreek leaves.

4. Cook uncovered for about 7 minutes, stirring occasionally.

5. Add the red chili powder and peas. Continue cooking for about 5 minutes. Stir in the dried mango powder, cream, garam masala and salt. Heat through before serving.

6. Serve with an Indian bread of your choice. *Serves 4*

Almond & Vegetable Curry

❊ Sabji Badam Kadhi

1. Prepare the vegetables: Separate the cauliflower into florets and blanch in boiling water for 2 minutes. Drain and set aside. Chop the bell peppers into bite-sized pieces and set aside. Peel and boil the potatoes until tender. Cut them into thin wedges and set aside.

2. Heat the oil in the same large skillet (or karahi) over medium-high heat. Add the onions and sauté until dark brown. Remove from the oil, drain on paper towels and transfer to a food processor. Purée the sautéed onions to a paste and set aside.

3. Add the almonds, red chilies, saffron, ginger and milk to the food processor and purée to a smooth paste. Set aside.

4. Heat the oil in a large, deep skillet over medium-high heat. Add the green peppers and sauté for 1 minute. Add the cauliflower and sauté for 4 minutes. Add the potatoes and fry until the vegetables turn golden brown, about 10 minutes.

5. Stir in the onion paste, sugar and salt.

6. Reduce the heat to medium-low and add the almond and chili paste; cook for 3 more minutes.

7. Whip the yogurt slightly with a whisk to remove any lumps. Add to the skillet. Cook for about 5 minutes, if required add a little milk to add moisture. Pour into a serving dish and garnish with fresh cream and cilantro. Serve hot. *Serves 4*

This is a Gujarati dish, full of the sweet, spicy and sour flavor that the locals love. Serve it for brunch with Puri (page 147) and pickles on the side.

1	small head of cauliflower
2–3	green bell peppers
2–3	large potatoes
¼ cup | 60 mL	oil
2	onions, diced
1 cup | 250 mL	almonds
6	red chilies
pinch	saffron threads
1 piece	ginger (½ inch/1 cm)
½ cup | 125 mL	milk
¼ cup | 60 mL	vegetable oil
1 tsp | 5 mL	sugar
to taste	salt
1½ cups | 375 mL	thick, plain yogurt
2 Tbsp | 30 mL	whipping cream (35%)
¼ cup | 60 mL	chopped cilantro

Potato Curry (*Alu Ki Bhaji*) 122

Bombay Potatoes (*Alu Mumbai Masala*) 123

Stuffed Potato Kebab (*Alu Kofta*) 124

Buttermilk Curry (*Gujarati Kadhi*) 125

Paneer Butter Masala (*Makhani Paneer*) 126

Spiced Vegetable Medley (*Sabzi Jalfrezi*) 128

Rajastani Spicy Okra (*Rajastani Bhindi Masala*) 129

Drumsticks in Sambaar (*Singhu Sambaar*) 130

Drumsticks with Potatoes (*Alu Singhu Masala*) 133

Spiced Roasted Eggplant (*Baigan Bhartha*) 135

Masala Eggplant (*Baigan Masala*) 136

Spicy Eggplant with Yogurt (*Dahi Baigan*) 137

Stuffed Eggplant Hyderabadi-Style (*Rawayya*) 138

Side Dishes

Potato Curry

❄ Alu Ki Bhaji

A tasty side dish that can be eaten with Puri (page 147), Paratha (page 145) or just plain rice. Accompany with Pickled Mangoes and Carrots (page 168) or Quick Mango Pickles (page 169).

1½ lb | 750 g	potatoes, preferably Idaho
6 Tbsp | 90 mL	oil
½ tsp | 2 mL	mustard seeds
3	red chilies
pinch	fenugreek seeds
½ lb | 250 g	onions, finely sliced
2	green chilies, chopped
1 tsp | 5 mL	turmeric
to taste	salt
½ cup | 125 mL	chopped cilantro
1 Tbsp | 15 mL	fresh lemon juice

1. Prepare the potatoes by washing them and placing them in a large saucepan of water over high heat. Boil them until tender, about 12–15 minutes (depending on the kind of potato). Allow them to cool. Peel and cut each one into small cubes. Set aside.

2. Heat the oil in a large, deep skillet (or karahi) over medium-high heat and add the mustard seeds. When the oil splutters, add the chilies and fenugreek seeds and reduce the heat to medium.

3. Immediately add the onions and green chilies. Fry until the onions are golden brown, about 4 minutes.

4. Add the turmeric, reserved potatoes and salt.

5. Sauté for about 10 minutes, or until heated through. Sprinkle with the chopped cilantro and lemon juice just before serving. *Serves 6*

Bombay Potatoes

Alu Mumbai Masala

1. If using new potatoes, bring a large saucepan of water to a boil, add the potatoes and cook until tender. Allow to cool, cut into bite-sized pieces and place in a large glass bowl. If using canned potatoes, cut the potatoes into bite-sized pieces and place in a glass bowl.

2. Add the red chili powder and sugar to the potatoes and toss to coat.

3. Heat the oil in a large, deep skillet (or karahi) over medium-high heat, then add the mustard seeds and curry leaves.

4. When the mustard seeds start to pop, add the garlic paste, paprika, turmeric and tomato paste. Sauté for about 10–15 seconds.

5. Add the potatoes to the pan, toss to coat and then add the lemon juice and water. Simmer for about 10 minutes, stirring occasionally. Season with salt and serve.
Serves 6

This simple and tasty Gujarati dish calls for new potatoes, but I have also used canned potatoes with excellent results. Serve as a side dish or just with Roti (page 144) or Naan (page 143).

12–15	new potatoes
	or
2	14 oz (398 mL) cans potatoes
½ tsp | 2 mL	red chili powder
1 tsp | 5 mL	sugar
¼ cup | 60 mL	vegetable oil
½ tsp | 2 mL	black mustard seeds
6–7	curry leaves
½ tsp | 2 mL	garlic paste (see page 177)
1 Tbsp | 15 mL	paprika
¾ tsp | 4 mL	turmeric
1 Tbsp | 15 mL	tomato paste
1 Tbsp | 15 mL	fresh lemon juice
½ cup | 125 mL	water
¼ tsp | 1 mL	salt

Stuffed Potato Kebab

❋ Alu Kofta

This dish, also known as tikkas, comes to you from the state of Gujarat. If you like heat, make it spicier by adding more red chili powder or green chili paste. Serve this as a snack or as a side dish with the chutney of your choice.

1 lb | 500 g	potatoes
2	slices day-old bread
1 tsp | 5 mL	ground roasted cumin seeds
to taste	red chili powder
to taste	salt
2	onions, chopped
½ cup | 125 mL	chopped mint
½ tsp | 2 mL	sugar
2	green chilies
½ cup | 125 mL	chopped cilantro
¼ tsp | 1 mL	garam masala (see page 173)
1 Tbsp | 15 mL	pomegranate seeds
to taste	salt
2 cups | 500 mL	breadcrumbs
2 cups | 500 mL	oil for frying

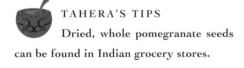

TAHERA'S TIPS

Dried, whole pomegranate seeds can be found in Indian grocery stores.

1. Peel the potatoes and cut them into chunks. Bring a large saucepan of water to a boil, add the potatoes and cook until tender, about 6–10 minutes. Drain and mash the potatoes. Set, aside to cool.

2. Soak the bread in water for about 2 minutes, then push the bread against a fine sieve to remove the water. Use the heel of your hand to squeeze out all the water you can.

3. In a large bowl, combine the potatoes, bread, cumin seeds, red chili powder and salt. Using your hands, knead until smooth. Set aside.

4. Purée the onions, mint, sugar, chilies, cilantro, garam masala, pomegranate seeds and salt in a food processor (do not add water). You should have a paste.

5. Place the breadcrumbs on a large plate. Set aside.

6. Place some of the potato mixture (about 2–3 Tbsp/ 30–45 mL) in the palm of your hand and flatten it.

7. Heat the oil in a large, deep skillet (or karahi) over high heat.

8. Place about 1 tsp (5 mL) of the onion paste in the center and roll the potato mixture around it. Roll the kebab in the breadcrumbs.

9. Drop the kebabs in the oil and deep-fry until golden brown, about 2 minutes. Make sure the oil is very hot so that they cook quickly. If you fry too long, they'll open up and absorb oil. Serve hot. *Serves 4–6*

Buttermilk Curry

❋ Gujarati Kadhi

1. In a small bowl, whisk together the yogurt, water, chana flour, ginger paste, jaggery and salt. Set aside.

2. Heat the oil in a large, deep skillet (or karahi). Add the mustard seeds. When they pop (after about 30 seconds), add the cumin seeds and curry leaves. Stir in the green chilies and asafetida and sauté for 1 minute.

3. Add the yogurt mixture, along with the cinnamon, whole cloves and fenugreek seeds. Cook, stirring constantly, until it comes to a boil. If the mixture becomes too runny, thicken it with chana flour combined with a bit of water.

4. Reduce the heat and cook for 5–8 minutes. Pour into a serving dish and sprinkle with the cilantro. *Serves 4–6*

TAHERA'S TIPS

Jaggery is a type of unrefined cane sugar that is sold in blocks. It is very popular in Gujarati cooking and you can find it at Indian as well as south Asian grocery stores.

A yogurt delicacy made famous by the Gujaratis, this curry is usually served with khichdi (try Royal Kedgeree on page 96), which is a mixture of rice and lentils. You can buy sour yogurt at an Indian grocery store, or you can make it by leaving your plain yogurt in the refrigerator for five days until it matures.

2 cups | 500 mL	sour yogurt
2 cups | 500 mL	water
2 Tbsp | 30 mL	chana flour (see page 18)
1 tsp | 5 mL	ginger paste (see page 176)
2 Tbsp | 30 mL	grated jaggery
to taste	salt
1 Tbsp | 15 mL	oil
1 tsp | 5 mL	mustard seeds
½ tsp | 2 mL	cumin seeds
2–3	curry leaves
2	green chilies, each split in half
¼ tsp | 1 mL	asafetida (see page 22)
¼	cinnamon stick (1 inch/2.5 cm)
5	whole cloves
¼ tsp | 1 mL	fenugreek seeds
¼ cup | 60 mL	chopped cilantro

Paneer Butter Masala

✳ Makhani Paneer

Indian housewives usually make fresh
paneer, but it is much easier to use the
ready-made version, especially if you're
new to Indian cooking. Paneer is sold in all
Indian grocery stores. If you'd really like
to try making it yourself, the recipe for this
unripened cheese can be found in my first
cookbook, Simply Indian. *Serve with rice
or Roti (page 144).*

2	onions, chopped
1 piece	ginger (1 inch/2.5 cm), chopped
2	garlic cloves, thinly sliced
4	tomatoes, roughly chopped
5 Tbsp	75 mL	vegetable oil
1 tsp	5 mL	red chili powder
½ cup	125 mL	milk
2 Tbsp	30 mL	chopped cashew nuts
¾ tsp	4 mL	roasted cumin powder
½ tsp	2 mL	garam masala (see page 173)
½ tsp	2 mL	sugar
to taste	salt
2 cups	500 mL	water
2 tsp	10 mL	fenugreek seeds
9 oz	270 g	paneer, cut into bite-sized pieces (see page 17)
2–3 drops	orange food coloring
2 Tbsp	30 mL	butter
1	green chili pepper, finely chopped
2	onions, cut into rings

1. Using a food processor, purée the onions, ginger and garlic to a paste. Remove and set aside. Then use the food processor to purée the tomatoes. Set aside.

2. Heat the oil in a large, deep skillet (or karahi) over medium-high heat. Add the onion paste and sauté until golden brown, about 2 minutes. Stir in the red chili powder and sauté for 1–2 minutes. Slowly add the milk, stirring to combine.

3. Add the cashews and reserved tomato purée and continue to cook for about 2–3 minutes. Then add the cumin powder, garam masala, sugar, salt and water. Cook until the oil separates and the gravy thickens, about 10 minutes.

4. Then add the fenugreek seeds, paneer and food coloring to the gravy and heat through.

5. In a separate small saucepan, heat the butter over medium-high heat. Add the green chili and onion rings. Sauté about 4 minutes. Add the sautéed green chilies and onions to the gravy; heat for a few minutes and serve hot. *Serves 4*

Spiced Vegetable Medley

✳ Sabzi Jalfrezi

This is a popular dish from Kashmir and Pakistan. Use fresh vegetables for the best results. Perfect for a brunch, lunch or an evening meal, it can be served with Naan (page 143), Paratha (page 145) or plain rice.

½	head of cauliflower
½ tsp | 2 mL	turmeric
3	medium potatoes
1 cup | 250 mL	vegetable oil
2	medium onions, thinly sliced
1	large carrot
1 cup | 250 mL	frozen peas
1	green bell pepper
1	red bell pepper
¼ cup | 60 mL	vegetable oil
8	fenugreek seeds
½ tsp | 2 mL	black onion seeds
10	curry leaves
¼ cup | 60 mL	curry masala paste (see page 174)
2 Tbsp | 30 mL	fresh lemon or lime juice
½ tsp | 2 mL	garam masala (see page 173)
½ tsp | 2 mL	salt

1. Prepare the vegetables: Separate the cauliflower into florets and blanch in boiling water with ½ tsp (2 mL) turmeric, about 3 minutes. Set aside. Peel and cube the potatoes and fry in the 1 cup (250 mL) of oil and set aside. Thinly slice the onion and set aside. Cut the carrot into 1-inch (2 cm) chunks and blanch in boiling water for about 6–8 minutes. Remove, drain and set aside. Microwave the peas on high for 3–4 minutes. Set aside. Chop the bell peppers and set aside.

2. Heat the ¼ cup (60 mL) oil in a large, deep skillet (or karahi) over medium-high heat. Add the fenugreek seeds and sauté for about 10–15 seconds. Stir in the black onion seeds and the curry leaves. Add the reserved onions and sauté for 3 minutes.

3. Add the curry masala paste and cook for about 2 minutes, until fragrant.

4. Add the reserved cauliflower, potatoes, carrot, peas, bell peppers and cook, stirring occasionally, for about 3 minutes. The vegetables should be slightly crunchy.

5. Add the lemon or lime juice, garam masala and salt. If the mixture is too dry, add up to ¼ cup (60 mL) of water. Serve hot. *Serves 4–6*

Rajastani Spicy Okra

❋ Rajastani Bhindi Masala

1. Wash the okra and place on a tea towel. Remove the ends and cut the pods into ¼-inch (6 mm) pieces. Set aside.

2. Combine the garlic, chilies and water in a food processor and purée to a smooth paste. Transfer to a small bowl and add the curry powder. Mix well and set aside.

3. Heat the oil in a large, deep skillet (or karahi) over medium-high heat. Add the okra and sauté for 3 minutes. Transfer to a paper towel to absorb excess oil.

4. Add the mustard seeds to the hot oil and sauté until they pop, about 30 seconds. Stir in the cumin seeds, then add the chopped onion. Sauté, stirring frequently until they become soft, roughly 4 or 5 minutes.

5. Return the okra to the mixture. Simmer for 3–4 minutes. Add the garam masala and the salt. Simmer, stirring gently so as not to break it up. Serve hot. *Serves 4*

Bhindi *is the Hindi name for okra, which is always fried in either vegetable oil or spicy soy oil. To better enhance the flavor of this dish, use young, tender okra pods. Serve it with Paratha (page 145) or Roti (page 144).*

1 lb	500 g	fresh okra pods
9	large cloves garlic
3	red Thai chilies
¼ cup	60 mL	water
1 tsp	5 mL	curry powder
½ cup	125 mL	vegetable oil
½ tsp	2 mL	mustard seeds
1 tsp	5 mL	roasted cumin seeds
1	large red onion, finely chopped
½ tsp	2 mL	garam masala (see page 173)
½ tsp	2 mL	salt
¼ cup	60 mL	chopped cilantro

Drumsticks in Sambaar

❋ *Singhu Sambaar*

Drumsticks have a sweet and distinct taste, adding a unique flavor to this sambaar, which is a word that usually describes a dish with a thick creamy sauce. This curry is usually enjoyed over rice or with dosas (page 156). It reminds me of my happy childhood days; my mum always served this with rice on Friday, which was known as daal day.

1 cup	250 mL	masoor daal
1	Japanese eggplant
6–7	tender drumsticks (see page 132)
1	large onion, finely chopped
2	tomatoes, finely chopped
2 cups	500 mL	water
¼ cup	60 mL	vegetable oil
pinch	black mustard seeds
6	curry leaves
½ tsp	2 mL	dried fenugreek leaves
1 piece	ginger (2 inches/5 cm), finely chopped
2 Tbsp	30 mL	grated fresh coconut
2 Tbsp	30 mL	curry masala paste (see page 174)
pinch	asafetida (see page 22)
¼ cup	60 mL	fresh lemon juice
to taste	salt
¼ cup	60 mL	chopped cilantro

1. Soak the masoor daal for 2 hours. Drain and set aside.

2. Cut the eggplant into ¼-inch (6 mm) rounds. Sprinkle them lightly with salt and leave for 10 minutes to become firm.

3. Scrape the sides of the drumsticks with a vegetable peeler or knife to partially remove the thicker, outer skin. Cut them into 3-inch (7.5 cm) pieces and parboil in salted water for about 7 minutes. Drain and set aside.

4. Combine the masoor daal, onion, tomatoes and water in a large saucepan over high heat and bring to a boil. Reduce the heat to low, cover it partly and cook for 15 minutes until the lentils are very soft.

5. Using a whisk, stir the mixture lightly for 2–3 minutes and add the drumsticks. Cook for another 20 minutes.

6. Heat the oil in large, deep skillet (or karahi) over medium-high heat and add the mustard seeds. When the seeds start to pop, stir in the curry and fenugreek leaves. Sauté for about 30 seconds.

7. Add the eggplant rounds and sear, turning occasionally, until both sides are almost brown.

(continued on page 132)

TAHERA'S TIPS

Drumsticks look similar to long green beans and are the pod of the moringa tree, which grows in tropical climates. Very common in southern India, this vegetable is also a favorite of Indians in East Africa. The outer skin is usually scraped off, then the vegetable is cut into pieces and parboiled in lightly salted water. It can be added to curries and sambaars, cooked with potatoes or even served with pancakes. Drumsticks are eaten like artichokes—the pulp is enjoyed and the rest discarded. Select tender drumstick pods that are light in color and thin-skinned.

8. Add the chopped ginger, fresh coconut and curry masala paste, stirring constantly to keep the mixture from sticking to the pan. Add the asafetida and lemon juice and mix well. Season with salt and simmer for 10 minutes.

9. Pour into a serving dish and garnish with the cilantro.
   Serves 4–6

To keep your cilantro fresh, trim about 3 inches off the stems and place the bunch in an airtight container with 2 raw eggs. It will keep in the refrigerator for about 10 days.

Drumsticks with Potatoes

❋ Alu Singhu Masala

1. Scrape the sides of the drumsticks with a vegetable peeler or knife to partially remove the thicker, outer skin. Cut them into 3-inch (7.5 cm) pieces and parboil in salted water for 8–10 minutes. Set aside.

2. Heat the oil in a large, deep skillet (or karahi) over medium-high heat, then add the mustard seeds and curry leaves. When the mustard seeds start to pop, add the onions and tomatoes and sauté for about 3 minutes.

3. Add the potatoes and cook for about 5 minutes. Add the red chili powder and curry masala paste and cook for another 3 minutes, stirring occasionally to make sure the mixture does not stick to the bottom of the pan.

4. Add the cauliflower and water and continue cooking for about 10 minutes, stirring occasionally or until the potatoes are almost tender.

5. Add the drumsticks, toss to coat and reduce the heat to low, stirring occasionally. The liquid should reduce enough to coat the potatoes, cauliflower and drumsticks. Pour into a serving dish and sprinkle with chopped cilantro. Serve hot. *Serves 4–6*

We used to eat this favorite Gujarati dish every Friday when drumsticks (singhu) were in season. We would almost always eat this crisp, tasty treat alongside grilled fish and Paratha (page 145).

4	tender drumsticks (see page 132)
¼ cup | 60 mL	vegetable oil
½ tsp | 2 mL	black mustard seeds
6	curry leaves
1	medium onion, finely chopped
3	tomatoes, finely chopped
10–12	new potatoes
¼ tsp | 1 mL	red chili powder
1 Tbsp | 15 mL	curry masala paste (see page 174)
1 small	cauliflower, cut into small florets
½ cup | 125 mL	water
¼ cup | 60 mL	chopped cilantro

CLOCKWISE FROM LEFT: *Roti* (page 144),
Spiced Roasted Eggplant (facing page),
Tomato Chutney (page 164),
Pickled Mangoes & Carrots (page 168),
Cauliflower & Pea Curry (page 113)

Spiced Roasted Eggplant

❋ Baigan Bhartha

1. Preheat the oven to 450°F (230°C).

2. Cut the eggplants in half lengthwise. Poke holes in the eggplants with a fork, rub lightly with some of the oil, place on a baking sheet and roast for about 40 minutes.

3. When the skin is charred and the flesh is softened, remove from the oven. Let cool slightly and remove the skin. Chop into big chunks and set aside in a glass bowl.

4. Heat the remaining oil in a large, deep skillet (or karahi) over medium-high heat. Add the onions and the garlic and ginger pastes. Reduce the heat to low and cook for 5–6 minutes until fragrant.

5. Add the paprika and chopped tomatoes. Continue cooking until a thick sauce forms. Add the cumin seeds, turmeric and green chilies.

6. Using a potato masher, mash the flesh of the eggplant until it is pulpy. Add it to the skillet and cook for at least 10 minutes, stirring often so it does not stick to the bottom. The oil should separate at the surface.

7. Add the salt and stir to combine. Place in a serving bowl and garnish with the chopped cilantro. *Serves 4*

TAHERA'S TIPS
For this dish, I usually use the large round eggplants rather than the Japanese eggplant since they are easier to mash and peel.

In this fantastic dish, the heat of the green chilies and the sweetness of the onions are nicely rounded out by the eggplants and tomatoes. If you want this dish a bit more spicy, you can leave the seeds in the green chilies. Serve with warm Roti (page 144) or on a bed of hot rice.

2	large eggplants
2 Tbsp | 30 mL	vegetable oil
2	medium sweet onions, finely chopped
1 tsp | 5 mL	garlic paste (see page 177)
1 tsp | 5 mL	ginger paste (see page 176)
1 tsp | 5 mL	paprika
2	large tomatoes, finely chopped
1 tsp | 5 mL	crushed roasted cumin seeds
½ tsp | 2 mL	turmeric
2	green chilies, seeded and chopped
½ tsp | 2 mL	sea salt
½ cup | 125 mL	chopped cilantro

Masala Eggplant

※ *Baigan Masala*

Eggplant is one of the most popular vegetables in Indian cooking. My aunt in Dubai was the one who taught me to make this typical Gujarati dish. Baigan is simply another name for eggplant.

2 cups | 500 mL	vegetable oil
10	purple baby eggplants
1 Tbsp | 15 mL	sesame seeds
2 Tbsp | 30 mL	peanuts
1 Tbsp | 15 mL	coriander seeds
½ cup | 125 mL	finely chopped onion
¼ cup | 60 mL	chopped tomatoes
1½ tsp | 7 mL	red chili powder
2 tsp | 10 mL	ginger paste (see page 176)
2 tsp | 10 mL	garlic paste (see page 177)
to taste	salt
2 tsp | 10 mL	grated jaggery (see page 125)
1 tsp | 5 mL	tamarind pulp (see page 38)
2 cups | 500 mL	water
1	large onion, slivered
¼ cup | 60 mL	chopped cilantro

1. Heat the oil in a large, deep skillet (or karahi) over medium-high heat. Remove the stems from the eggplants and slice them lengthwise. Deep-fry until golden brown, about 2 minutes. Place on paper towels to drain.

2. In a small skillet, combine the sesame seeds, peanuts and coriander seeds and dry-roast over medium-high heat, or just until the sesame seeds are golden brown. Grind in a coffee grinder or mortar and pestle and set aside.

3. Remove most of the oil from the large skillet that you used for deep-frying, leaving about ¼ cup (60 mL). Heat over medium-high heat and sauté the onion until golden brown, about 4 minutes. Remove from the pan and pulse in a food processor to a coarse paste.

4. Add the tomatoes to the skillet and sauté until the mixture is pulpy. Add the puréed onion paste, red chili powder, ginger and garlic pastes, salt, jaggery and tamarind pulp. Cook for 3–4 minutes. Stir in the roasted sesame and peanut powder.

5. Add the water and when it starts boiling add the deep-fried eggplants. Cook until the gravy becomes thick and the eggplant is heated through.

6. Pour into a serving dish and garnish with the onions and cilantro before serving. *Serves 4–6*

Spicy Eggplant with Yogurt

❀ Dahi Baigan

1. Chop the eggplant into bite-sized chunks and place in a glass bowl. Add the salt, turmeric, red chili powder, lime juice, ginger and garlic pastes and toss to coat. Marinate in the refrigerator for 30 minutes.

2. Heat the oil in a large, deep skillet (or karahi) over medium-high heat. Add the chopped eggplant and sauté until it is golden-brown, about 5 minutes. Remove from the skillet and set aside.

3. Heat the ghee in the same large skillet over medium-high heat. When it is hot, add the curry leaves and onions. Sauté for about 30 seconds. Add the fenugreek seeds, mustard seeds, anise seeds, cumin, coriander seeds, green chilies, turmeric and salt. Sauté for about 1 minute until fragrant. Reduce the heat to low.

4. In a small bowl, whisk together the flour, yogurt and water to reach a thick, saucy consistency. Add the yogurt to the skillet with the eggplant, increase the heat to medium-high and return a boil.

5. Garnish with cilantro and serve. *Serves 4–6*

Eggplant cooked with yogurt is popular throughout India, but perhaps nowhere more so than in Punjab. Here it is marinated in spices, then fried. Serve with Roti (page 144) or Puri (page 147).

1 lb | 500 g	eggplant
to taste	salt
1 tsp | 5 mL	turmeric
½ tsp | 2 mL	red chili powder
2 Tbsp | 30 mL	fresh lime juice
1 tsp | 5 mL	ginger paste (see page 176)
1 tsp | 5 mL	garlic paste (see page 177)
¼ cup | 60 mL	vegetable oil
1 Tbsp | 15 mL	ghee (clarified butter)
8–10	curry leaves
2	onions, finely chopped
½ tsp | 2 mL	fenugreek seeds
½ tsp | 2 mL	mustard seeds
1½ tsp | 7 mL	anise seeds
½ tsp | 2 mL	ground cumin
1 tsp | 5 mL	coriander seeds
1 tsp | 5 mL	green chilies, chopped
½ tsp | 2 mL	turmeric
to taste	salt
1 Tbsp | 15 mL	all-purpose flour
1 cup | 250 mL	plain yogurt
¼ cup | 60 mL	water
¼ cup | 60 mL	chopped cilantro

Stuffed Eggplant Hyderabadi-Style

✳ Rawayya

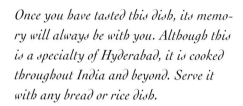

Once you have tasted this dish, its memory will always be with you. Although this is a specialty of Hyderabad, it is cooked throughout India and beyond. Serve it with any bread or rice dish.

7–8	baby eggplants
1 Tbsp | 15 mL	garlic paste (see page 177)
1 Tbsp | 15 mL	curry masala paste (see page 174)
1 tsp | 5 mL	coarsely ground roasted cumin seeds
1 tsp | 5 mL	poppy seeds
1 Tbsp | 15 mL	onion purée (see page 177)
1 tsp | 5 mL	coarsely ground roasted coriander
1 Tbsp | 15 mL	unsweetened desiccated coconut
1 tsp | 5 mL	sesame seeds
2 Tbsp | 30 mL	tamarind pulp (see page 38)
½ tsp | 2 mL	sea salt
¼ cup | 60 mL	vegetable oil
1 tsp | 5 mL	black mustard seeds
7–8	curry leaves
1	large onion, sliced
2 Tbsp | 30 mL	chopped cilantro

1. Starting at the bottom, slice each eggplant into quarters lengthwise, but stop 1 inch (2.5 cm) from the stem so the eggplants stay intact at the stem end.

2. In a medium-sized bowl, combine the garlic paste, curry masala paste, cumin seeds, poppy seeds, onion purée, coriander, coconut, sesame seeds, 1 Tbsp (15 mL) of the tamarind pulp and salt.

3. Smear 2–3 tsp (10–15 mL) of the mixture inside and over the surface of each eggplant. Set the remainder aside; it will be used later in the recipe.

4. Heat the oil in a large, deep skillet (or karahi) over medium-high heat. Add the mustard seeds and, when they start to pop (about 30 seconds), add the curry leaves and sliced onion. Sauté until the onion starts to turn golden brown.

5. Add the reserved spice mixture and sauté for 3–4 minutes until fragrant.

6. Lower the eggplants carefully into the skillet and baste them with the spiced mixture and onions.

7. Place the lid on tightly and reduce the heat, allowing to simmer until the eggplants are cooked, about 10–12 minutes.

8. Set the eggplants on a serving platter; garnish with the cilantro and drizzle with the remaining tamarind pulp. Serve hot. *Serves 4–6*

Naan 143

Roti (*Chapati*) 144

Paratha 145

Yogurt Paratha (*Dahi Paratha*) 146

Puri 147

Millet Bread (*Dhebra*) 148

Cheese Bread 149

African Donuts (*Mandazi*) 150

Bengali Bread (*Luchis*) 153

Afghanistani Sweet Bread 154

Onion Bread (*Pesarattu*) 155

Onion Dosas 157

Coconut Dosas 158

Naan, Roti & Breads

North, West and East Pakistan, Rajasthan and Punjab are famous for their tandoori naan (oven-baked bread). Skillet breads include roti and phulka and the famous bhatura, as well as other breads from the naan family. You can find more recipes for these in my first book, *Simply Indian*.

These breads are sometimes flavored with yogurt and a variety of herbs. Other times, a spiced potato mixture is introduced into the dough when kneading or rolling it out. They are best if thoroughly kneaded and left to rest for at least 2 hours or even longer before being rolled out, then cooked on medium-high heat in a cast-iron skillet or a flat cast-iron pan used for making bread, called a tava.

The breads of Afghanistan are similar to those of Pakistan, India and Iran. There are a dozen different types to satisfy all tastes—the soft thin breads accompany kebabs, while the thicker ones are served with olives and feta cheese.

Try different breads with your dishes. Don't be afraid to try eating a sweet bread with a spicy dish. The sweetness tends to tone down the spiciness in some dishes.

Naan

1. In a large bowl, mix together the yeast, sugar and warm water and let sit for 5 minutes.

2. Add the flour, salt, milk powder, vegetable oil and beaten egg to the bowl and mix well.

3. Add the yogurt and, using your hands, gradually work all the ingredients together to form a soft pliable dough.

4. Knead vigorously and cover with a moistened tea towel. Leave in a warm place to rise to just less than double its size, about 2 hours.

5. Dust your hands with plenty of flour and shape dough into 6 large balls.

6. Make each ball into a oval-shaped pancake by gently rolling them out and pulling the dough gently.

7. Brush the top of each naan with melted butter and the bottom with milk and place in frying pan. If desired, scatter sesame seeds on top.

8. Broil each naan on high to cook the top part, then remove and cook in a skillet on the stove to cook the bottom part. This will take 2–3 minutes and once cooked the naan will slide easily out of the frying pan. *Makes 6 large naan*

Traditionally, naan is baked in clay ovens called tandoors, but this recipe uses a conventional oven and stovetop. Naan originates from the Punjab and usually accompanies tandoori meat dishes and vegetable dishes very well.

2¼ tsp | 8 g	instant yeast (1 package)
1 tsp | 5 mL	sugar
½ cup | 125 mL	warm water
2½ cups | 625 mL	all-purpose flour
1 tsp | 5 mL	salt
5 Tbsp | 75 mL	milk powder
¼ cup | 60 mL	vegetable oil
1	egg, beaten
5 Tbsp | 75 mL	plain yogurt
2 Tbsp | 30 mL	melted butter
2 Tbsp | 30 mL	warm milk
	sesame seeds (optional)

Roti

Chapati

Also known as chapati, this traditional unleavened Indian flatbread can accompany almost every meal of the day. Roti is different from naan bread in several ways: it is an unleavened quick bread, it is cooked on a skillet or a tawa, and the main ingredient is atta flour, a whole wheat flour. Roti should be made 30 minutes before serving, and they complement any curry.

2 cups | 500 mL	atta flour
1 tsp | 5 mL	salt
3 Tbsp | 45 mL	ghee (clarified butter)
2 cups | 500 mL	water

1. In a large bowl, combine the atta flour and salt. Add 2 Tbsp (20 mL) of the ghee and combine using your hands.

2. Slowly pour in the water and knead the dough till it become soft. Cover and set aside for about 1 hour.

3. After 1 hour, add about ½ tsp (2 mL) of the remaining ghee and knead the dough again. Roll out the dough into small balls, about the size of golf balls.

4. Flatten each ball and sprinkle lightly on both sides with atta flour. Sprinkle atta flour on your rolling surface. Roll out each roti until it is about 8 inches (20 cm) in diameter.

5. Heat a skillet or tawa over medium-high heat. Don't add oil to the pan. Place the roti on the skillet and cook until slightly spotted on both sides.

6. When done, take the roti off the hot pan and brush lightly with the remaining ghee. *Makes 5–6 roti*

Paratha

1. Sift the flour into a large bowl, then add the salt and the ¼ cup (60 mL) oil. Mix well.

2. Add enough water to make a soft elastic dough that is not sticky when kneaded.

3. Divide the dough into 8 balls.

4. On a floured surface roll out each ball until it is approximately 8 inches (20 cm) in diameter. Brush the surface of each paratha with a bit of the 2 Tbsp (30 mL) of oil and sprinkle lightly with flour.

5. Fold in half, then in half again. Roll out thinly. Brush the surface again with oil and sprinkle lightly with flour.

6. Heat a skillet or tawa on medium heat and cook one paratha at a time, placing a little oil along the edges.

7. Cook the paratha on each side until golden brown. Serve hot. *Makes 8 paratha*

This griddle-cooked bread is a richer, softer and flakier variation of chapatis. Serve it with any curry.

2½ cups	625 mL	whole wheat flour
½ tsp	2 mL	salt
¼ cup	60 mL	vegetable oil
¾ cup	185 mL	water
2 Tbsp	30 mL	vegetable oil

Yogurt Paratha

❋ *Dahi Paratha*

*Dahi Paratha makes a delicious accom-
paniment to any daal dish. This version
has yogurt in it. If you prepare paratha
ahead of time, wrap them in foil and
place them inside a warm oven. This will
keep them soft and moist. Dahi Paratha
can also be frozen in foil.*

4 cups ǀ 1 L	all-purpose flour
1 tsp ǀ 5 mL	sugar
1 tsp ǀ 5 mL	baking powder
½ tsp ǀ 2 mL	salt
½ cup ǀ 125 mL	vegetable oil
1	egg, beaten
½ cup ǀ 125 mL	plain yogurt
½ cup ǀ 125 mL	all-purpose flour
¼ cup ǀ 60 mL	vegetable oil

1. In a large bowl, combine the flour with the sugar, baking powder and salt. Add the ½ cup (125 mL) of oil and
   mix well.

2. Add the egg and yogurt and knead to form dough. Set
   aside, covered, for 2 hours.

3. Divide the dough into about 6 balls, each about the size
   of a golf ball or slightly bigger.

4. Flatten the balls and sprinkle both sides lightly with the
   ½ cup (125 mL) of flour.

5. Roll out to about 12 inches (30 cm) in diameter.

6. Heat a skillet or tawa over medium heat and cook one
   paratha at a time placing a little of the ¼ cup (60 mL) oil
   along the edges.

7. Cook the paratha on each side until golden brown.
   Serve hot. *Makes 5–6 paratha*

Puri

1. Mix together the flour, salt and oil and rub together with your hands until the mixture resembles coarse breadcrumbs.

2. Form into dough by adding small amounts of water and kneading until it makes a soft pliable dough.

3. Divide the dough into 10 small balls, each about the size of golf balls.

4. Roll each ball of dough out to about 1½ inches (4 cm) in diameter.

5. Heat the 2 cups (500 mL) of oil in a large, deep skillet (or karahi) over medium-high heat. Deep-fry about 3 at a time, tapping them with a spoon until they puff up and turn golden brown, about 40 seconds. *Makes 10 puri*

Puri is central India's equivalent of the North's roti. These unleavened puffed breads are usually deep-fried. Serve these with any vegetable curry, or for breakfast lunch or dinner. You can make your own variations by stuffing with vegetables, daals or even ground beef. Put 1 tsp (5 mL) of stuffing in the middle of the dough, then seal it up and deep-fry.

1 cup	250 mL	all-purpose flour
¼ tsp	1 mL	salt
1 Tbsp	15 mL	vegetable oil
⅓ cup	80 mL	water
2 cups	500 mL	oil for deep-frying

Millet Bread

✳ Dhebra

A specialty of Gujarat state, Dhebra is a kind of roti made with a blend of atta (a kind of whole wheat flour) and bajri (millet flour). This is the perfect bread for Sunday brunches or picnics. Serve it with yogurt or Raita (page 169).

1 cup | 250 mL	atta flour
1 cup | 250 mL	millet flour
¾ tsp | 4 mL	sea salt
2 Tbsp | 30 mL	vegetable oil
¾ tsp | 4 mL	garlic paste (see page 177)
1 tsp | 5 mL	fenugreek seeds
2	green chilies, finely chopped
1 tsp | 5 mL	turmeric
1 tsp | 5 mL	sugar
1 cup | 250 mL	plain yogurt
½ cup | 125 mL	water
1 cup | 250 mL	vegetable oil

1. Combine the two flours, salt, vegetable oil, garlic paste, fenugreek seeds, green chilies, turmeric and sugar in a large bowl.

2. Mix well and then add the yogurt. Knead until the mixture forms a soft, pliable dough, about 10 minutes. If the mixture is too dry, add some of the water, a little at a time, until you can form a nice, soft dough.

3. Cover with a moist cloth and let stand for 1 hour in a warm place.

4. Form into 6 small balls, each about the size of a golf ball, and roll out flat. Each dhebra will be about 4–5 inches (10–12 cm) across.

5. Heat a nonstick skillet over medium-high heat and place a dhebra in the pan. Add vegetable oil in drops around the dhebra. Fry until golden brown on both sides. *Makes about 6 pieces*

Cheese Bread

1. Combine the flour, yeast, salt, oil and sugar in a large mixing bowl. Add the water little by little, kneading to make a soft and pliable dough.

2. Cover the bowl with a moist tea towel or plastic wrap and put it in a warm place until it doubles in size, about 1½–2 hours.

3. While the bread is resting, grate the cheeses and put them in a large bowl. Add the flour and baking powder. Stir in the mint and 2 of the beaten eggs and mix to combine.

4. Preheat the oven to 350°F (180°C). Divide the dough into balls about the size of eggs and roll them out into round discs.

5. Place about 1 Tbsp (15 mL) of the cheese filling in the center of each disc. Pull the dough around the cheese filling by pulling up at 3 or 4 points to make a rectangle. Pinch the 4 corners together to seal and place on a baking sheet to rise, about ½ hour. You should still be able to see the cheese filling in the middle.

6. Just before baking, brush with the beaten egg and sprinkle the sesame seeds over the bread.

7. Bake for 12–15 minutes, or until golden brown and the cheese filling is puffed up. Serve warm. *Makes about 25 pieces*

I like to serve this Middle Eastern–style cheese bread with green olives and black coffee on a cold day.

4 cups	1 L	all-purpose flour
2¼ tsp	8 g	instant yeast
1 tsp	5 mL	salt
2 Tbsp	30 mL	olive oil or vegetable oil
2 tsp	10 mL	sugar
¾ cup	185 mL	water
8 oz	250 g	cheddar cheese
4 oz	125 g	halloumi cheese
1 cup	250 mL	all-purpose flour
1 tsp	5 mL	baking powder
1 Tbsp	15 mL	dried mint
2	eggs, beaten
1	egg, beaten (for egg wash)
½ cup	125 mL	sesame seeds

TAHERA'S TIPS
Halloumi cheese can be found in Middle Eastern delis. It's a rubbery hard cheese that you can fry without it melting.

African Donuts

※ *Mandazi*

Mandazis are a puffed, semisweet bread, usually deep-fried, that are very common in East Africa, especially on the island of Zanzibar. They can be served alone, with tea or with Pigeon Peas in Coconut Sauce (page 110).

6½ cups | 1.75 L	all-purpose flour
6 Tbsp | 90 mL	vegetable oil
1 cup | 250 mL	sugar
1	egg, beaten
3½ tsp | 17 mL	instant yeast
2 tsp | 20 mL	custard powder
¾ tsp | 4 mL	coarsely ground cardamom
1½ cups | 375 mL	water
4 cups | 1 L	oil for deep-frying

1. Mix the flour, vegetable oil, sugar, egg, yeast, custard powder and ground cardamom together in a large mixing bowl.

2. Add the water gradually, working it into the mixture to form a soft pliable dough. Turn it out on to a work surface and knead thoroughly with your fingertips. It should stay very soft and springy.

3. Cover with a moistened tea towel and place in a warm place to rise for about 3 hours. It will almost double in size.

4. Knead once more for 4–5 minutes and then roll the dough into a large rectangle about ½ inch (1 cm) thick.

5. Cut into strips about 3 inches (7.5 cm) wide and cut the strips into either squares or triangles.

(continued on page 152)

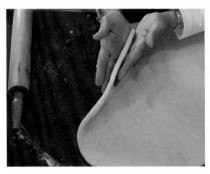

African Donuts (facing page)
served with Pigeon Peas in Coconut Sauce (page 110)

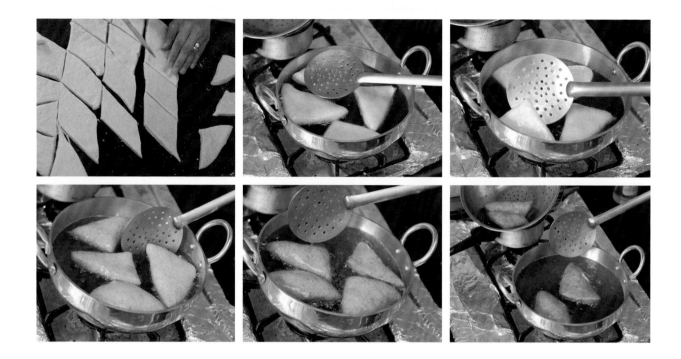

6. Sprinkle some extra flour on a flat surface and lay the dough pieces out to rise for about 15 minutes.

7. Heat the oil in a large, deep skillet (or karahi) over medium-high heat. When it's hot, deep-fry the mandazi on both sides, tapping them with a slotted spoon until they puff up and turn golden brown. Drain on paper towels. *Serves 4–6*

Bengali Bread

1. In a food processor, combine 3 cups (750 mL) of the flour, the salt and the 3 tablespoons (45 mL) of oil and process on low speed.

2. Gradually add the water to form a soft pliable dough (you may not need all the water).

3. Turn the dough onto a lightly floured surface using a little of the remaining 1 cup (250 mL) of flour. Knead for about 10 minutes until a very soft, smooth dough is formed.

4. Cover the dough with a moist tea towel or plastic wrap and leave for 2–3 hours in a warm place. If you don't have time to let it rest that long, leave it for at least 30 minutes.

5. Divide the dough into 10 equal parts about the size of golf balls.

6. Place the balls on a slightly floured surface and flatten with a rolling pin into circles about 4 inches (10 cm) in diameter.

7. Heat the 3 cups (750 mL) oil in a large, deep skillet (or karahi) over medium-high heat.

8. Fry each luchi; using a slotted spoon, gently tap on them until they puff up and turn golden brown. Cook on both sides. Place on a paper towel to drain. Serve warm.
Makes 10 luchis

This is a deep-fried, puffed Bengali bread made with all-purpose flour. The best results are achieved with a lot of kneading and a resting time (at least 2 hours) before rolling out the luchis. Enjoy them with Raita (page 169) and any vegetable dish.

4 cups | 1 L	all-purpose flour
½ tsp | 2 mL	salt
3 Tbsp | 45 mL	vegetable oil
1½ cups | 375 mL	cold water
3 cups | 750 mL	oil for deep-frying

Afghanistani Sweet Bread

The soft sweet breads of Afghanistan are great with tea or coffee. Whole wheat flour is usually used and the bread is leavened with a fermented starter. However, it's not easy to know how to handle such a starter, so in this recipe I have used yeast.

1¼ tsp | 6 mL	instant yeast
¼ cup | 60 mL	warm water
3 cups | 750 mL	whole wheat flour
1 cup | 250 mL	all-purpose flour
¾ tsp | 4 mL	sea salt
¼ cup | 60 mL	warm vegetable oil
1 cup | 250 mL	sugar
½ tsp | 2 mL	freshly ground cardamom
¼ cup | 60 mL	whole milk

TAHERA'S TIPS

To make a Pakistani version called Sheermaal, melt 1 Tbsp (15 mL) of butter in the skillet before adding the dough. Sprinkle caster sugar on each Sheermaal before serving.

1. Sprinkle the yeast on top of the water and set aside for 7 minutes.

2. Mix both the flours and the salt in a large mixing bowl. Add the oil, rubbing it in with your finger tips until the mixture resembles fine breadcrumbs.

3. Add the yeast mixture, then the sugar and ground cardamom and mix well.

4. Add the milk little by little and knead well until an elastic dough forms, about 10 minutes.

5. Cover with a damp cloth and set aside to rise for at least 2–3 hours or until almost double in size.

6. Divide the dough into 6 equal parts and form into balls.

7. Working with one ball at a time, roll out the dough with a rolling pin into a round or oval shape about ¼ inch (6 mm) thick. Use a fork to prick holes in the bread to prevent it from bubbling up.

8. Heat a skillet or tawa over medium-high heat. Don't add oil to the pan. Place the dough on the skillet and cook until slightly spotted. Turn and cook the other side for a further 1–2 minutes. Repeat with the remaining dough.

9. Place the breads in a slightly damp tea towel and serve hot with the curry of your choice. *Makes 6 pieces*

Onion Bread

❋ Pesarattu

1. Combine the daal and fenugreek seeds with the 4 cups (1 L) water in a large bowl and let soak overnight. The next day, drain and purée into a gritty paste using a food processor or a hand-held mixer.

2. Add the salt, green chilies, chopped ginger and the 1 cup (250 mL) of water and blend again for 1 minute. This batter shouldn't be too runny.

3. Heat 1 Tbsp (15 mL) of the oil in a skillet over medium-high heat and tilt to coat the skillet.

4. When the oil is hot, drop in just a few black mustard seeds (about a pinch). When the seeds begin to pop, spread a ladleful of batter evenly over the pan.

5. Immediately sprinkle 1 Tbsp (15 mL) of chopped onions, a pinch of roasted ground cumin seeds and then a handful of chopped cilantro over the batter.

6. Cook for 2 minutes, flip and cook on the other side for 2 minutes. Transfer to a plate and cover with a tea towel to keep warm. Repeat with the remaining batter and ingredients. *Makes 6–8 pieces*

Originating in Andhra Pradesh, this crêpe-like skillet bread is also popular in Hyderabad and is sometimes served for breakfast with Spiced Roasted Eggplant (page 135). Because it is made from a batter and not a dough, it's generally enjoyed hot. It's very similar to dosas, but it's made with beans not rice. Remember, because you need to soak the urad daal, you have to start this recipe the day before you're going to serve it.

1½ cups | 375 mL	urad daal
6–8	fenugreek seeds
4 cups | 1 L	warm water
1 tsp | 5 mL	sea salt
2	green chilies, chopped
1 piece	ginger (2 inches/5 cm), chopped
1 cup | 250 mL	water
6 Tbsp | 90 mL	vegetable oil
1 tsp | 5 mL	black mustard seeds
1	large onion, chopped
1 tsp | 5 mL	roasted ground cumin seeds
1 bunch	cilantro, chopped

DOSAS

In the south of India the dosa is very popular, particularly as a breakfast item. It is like a crêpe made from a batter of urad daal (white lentils) and rice that is left to ferment for a day before being cooked. There are hundreds of ways to make and serve dosas, and they are the perfect food for those who may be allergic to wheat or gluten.

TIPS FOR MAKING DOSAS

There are many griddles on the market, including cast-iron ones, but I find my nonstick frying pan takes the worry out of dosas as well as many other foods. When making dosas, the frying pan should be hot enough that a few drops of water will evaporate immediately. Reduce the heat and brush oil on the pan with a piece of paper towel with vegetable oil on it.

Dosa batter should be of a pouring consistency, just like a crêpe batter. Add a little more rice flour if the batter is too thin. The batter should be at room temperature. If you have kept it in the refrigerator, allow it time to return to room temperature before making dosas.

Onion Dosas

1. Place the daals in 3 separate bowls. Combine the rice and fenugreek in another bowl. Cover all with cold water and soak overnight.

2. The next day, drain and purée each ingredient separately. Process each to a smooth paste by blending with a little water. Then combine the daals and the rice pastes together in a large bowl and add the salt. The mixture should be the consistency of crêpe batter.

3. Using the same blender, process the onion, coconut, chili paste and ginger into a paste. You may have to add a little water to make a paste. Add it to the bowl and mix well with the daal-rice mixture.

4. Add the asafetida and all but ¼ cup (60 mL) of the chopped cilantro. The mixture should be of a pouring consistency; if it is too thin, add a little rice flour to thicken it.

5. Heat a few drops of the oil in a large nonstick skillet over medium-high heat. Spread a ladleful of batter to the skillet and tilt to coat. Quickly sprinkle some cilantro on top. Cover with a lid and cook until bubbles form on the surface and the bottom is browned, about 2–3 minutes.

6. Turn and cook on the other side for about 40 minutes. Repeat until all the batter is used. Serve hot. *Makes 10–12 dosas*

This is another specialty of South India. These pancakes are quite spicy and don't need any filling. You can serve them with or without chutney, but Mango Chutney (page 163) goes especially well with these dosas.

1 cup | 250 mL	chana daal
½ cup | 125 mL	mung daal
½ cup | 125 mL	toor daal (see page 110)
¾ cup | 185 mL	basmati rice
8	fenugreek seeds
½ tsp | 2 mL	sea salt
3	large onions, chopped
3 Tbsp | 45 mL	unsweetened desiccated coconut
2 tsp | 10 mL	chili paste (sambal olek)
1 piece	ginger (2 inches/5 cm), finely chopped
1 tsp | 5 mL	asafetida (see page 22)
1 bunch	cilantro, chopped
2 Tbsp | 30 mL	vegetable oil

Coconut Dosas

Coconut dosas consist of two main ingredients—rice and grated coconut—and form the basis of a southern Indian meal. In a vegetarian meal, the filling is usually made of potatoes, but this recipe is a nonvegetarian version. My preference is to use chicken, but you can use any meat. Note that you'll need to start this dish the day before you are going to serve it.

BATTER

1½ cups | 375 mL	basmati rice
8	fenugreek seeds
1	grated fresh coconut
1 piece	ginger (2 inches/5 cm), finely chopped
4	cloves garlic
2 Tbsp | 30 mL	chopped cilantro
2	green chilies, seeded and roughly chopped
1 tsp | 5 mL	chopped curry leaves
½ cup | 125 mL	water
½ tsp | 2 mL	sea salt

FOR THE BATTER

1. Wash and soak the rice and fenugreek seeds overnight in a bowl of water.

2. The next day, drain the rice. Combine the rice, fenugreek seeds, coconut, ginger, garlic, cilantro, green chilies and curry leaves in a food processor or blender.

3. Blend to a smooth paste. Add the water a little at a time to make a smooth batter. Add the salt and refrigerate the batter in a glass container for 1 day.

FOR THE CHICKEN FILLING

1. In a large skillet over medium-high heat, add the ground chicken, garlic and ginger pastes, green chili and lemon juice, stirring continuously to break up any lumps.

2. When all the liquid has evaporated and the meat is cooked through and dry, stir in the chopped onions and turn the heat off. Add the chopped cilantro, salt and garam masala. Mix thoroughly and set aside.

FOR THE CHUTNEY

1. Roast the chana daal in a skillet over medium-high heat, stirring constantly until it's browned, about 4–5 minutes.

2. Place the daal, oil, chopped onion, red chili powder, tamarind pulp, mint leaves, water and salt in a food processor or blender and process until it becomes a nice smooth paste.

TO ASSEMBLE

1. Heat a little of the vegetable oil in a large nonstick skillet over medium-high heat and spread a ladle of batter evenly on it. Tilt to coat the skillet.

2. Cover with a lid and cook until bubbles start to form on the top of the dosa and the bottom is brown, about 2½–3 minutes.

3. Flip the dosa over and cook just slightly on the other side, about 40 seconds.

4. Remove from the pan, top with 1½ tsp (7 mL) of the chutney and 1½ Tbsp (22 mL) of the meat filling. Fold the dosa in half and serve hot. Serve these immediately, otherwise they become soggy. Repeat until all the batter and filling is used. *Makes 10 dosas*

CHICKEN FILLING

1½ lb	750 g	ground chicken
1 tsp	5 mL	garlic paste (see page 177)
1 tsp	5 mL	ginger paste (see page 176)
1	green chili, seeded and chopped
2 Tbsp	30 mL	fresh lemon juice
2	large onions, finely chopped
½ cup	125 mL	chopped cilantro
½ tsp	2 mL	sea salt
½ tsp	2 mL	garam masala (see page 173)

CHUTNEY

1½ cups	375 mL	chana daal
1 Tbsp	15 mL	vegetable oil
1	large onion, chopped
½ tsp	2 mL	red chili powder
5 Tbsp	75 mL	tamarind pulp (see page 38)
1 bunch	mint
1 cup	250 mL	water
½ tsp	2 mL	sea salt
1 Tbsp	15 mL	vegetable oil (for frying)

Fresh Green Chutney (*Lila Chatni*) 162

Date & Tamarind Chutney (*Khajur Imli Chatni*) 162

Mango Chutney (*Aam Chatni*) 163

Red Coconut Chutney (*Laal Nariyal Chatni*) 163

Tomato Chutney (*Tamatar Chatni*) 164

Nushi's Tangy Chutney 165

Mango Pickles (*Keri Ka Achaar*) 166

Pickled Mangoes & Carrots (*Sambaro*) 168

Quick Mango Pickles (*Aam Achaar*) 169

Raita 169

Chutneys & Pickles

Fresh Green Chutney

❋ *Lila Chatni*

Spicy chutneys can give a kick to the taste buds, but you can adjust the spices and green chilies to your taste. This chutney is not only a good complement to many dishes, but it is also perfect for mixing with a yogurt base or sour cream for marinating.

1 bunch	cilantro, chopped
8	long Indian chilies, chopped
8	large cloves of garlic, finely chopped
1 piece	ginger (2 inches/5 cm), finely chopped
1 bunch	green onions, chopped
1½ tsp | 7 mL	roasted cumin seeds, coarsely ground
1 tsp | 5 mL	lemon zest
¼ cup | 60 mL	fresh lemon juice
1 cup | 250 mL	unsweetened desiccated coconut
1 tsp | 5 mL	sea salt
1½ tsp | 7 mL	sugar

1. Combine all the ingredients in a food processor or blender and process until smooth.

2. Transfer to a nonreactive container and refrigerate for 1 hour before serving. This chutney keep for up to 5 days in the refrigerator. *Makes 2 cups (500 mL)*

Date & Tamarind Chutney

❋ *Khajur Imli Chatni*

Versions of this chutney are served at most dinner tables in India and Pakistan. Serve with kebabs or stuffed paratha. The pitted and chopped dates are available in most Mediterranean supermarkets.

½ lb | 250 g	pitted and chopped dates
2 Tbsp | 30 mL	tamarind pulp (see page 38)
2 Tbsp | 30 mL	ketchup
1½ tsp | 7 mL	grated fresh ginger
1 tsp | 5 mL	ground coriander
1 tsp | 5 mL	red chili powder
1 Tbsp | 15 mL	sugar
1 Tbsp | 15 mL	chopped mint
to taste	salt
1 cup | 250 mL	water
1 sprig	mint leaves (for garnish)

1. Combine all the ingredients except the mint leaves in a food processor or blender and process until smooth.

2. Transfer to a nonreactive container and refrigerate for 1 hour before serving.

3. Garnish with a small sprig of mint leaves. This chutney keeps for up to 5 days in the refrigerator. *Makes about 3 cups (750 mL)*

Mango Chutney

Aam Chatni

This chutney is one of India's most loved digestives because it really triggers a failing appetite. If you want to tone down the spiciness, use slightly ripe mangoes, or add 1 tsp (5 mL) sugar to give it a sweeter taste.

3	green mangoes
2	green chilies, deseeded and chopped
1 tsp | 5 mL	salt
1 Tbsp | 15 mL	chopped mint

1. Peel the mangoes and chop into small pieces.
2. Place the mangoes, green chilies, salt and mint in a food processor or blender and process until smooth.
3. Transfer to a nonreactive container. This chutney keeps in the refrigerator for up to 5 days. *Makes about 3 cups (750 mL)*

Red Coconut Chutney

Laal Nariyal Chatni

This East Indian chutney is served mainly with starters, such as kebabs, pakoras and samosas. Try it with pilaus and you'll love it too.

4	whole red Thai or Indian chilies
1 cup | 250 mL	unsweetened desiccated coconut
2	cloves garlic
½ tsp | 2 mL	salt
2 Tbsp | 30 mL	fresh lemon or lime juice
½ cup | 125 mL	water

1. Wash the chilies and remove the stalks. Don't chop them.
2. Combine the chilies, coconut, salt, lemon or lime juice and water in a food processor or blender and process until smooth.
3. Transfer to a nonreactive container. This chutney keeps in the refrigerator for up to 5 days. *Makes about 1½ cups (375 mL)*

Tomato Chutney

❊ Tamatar Chatni

This is the kind of chutney that is made fresh in our homes three times a week. Those of you who like it spicy can increase the amount of chilies and ginger. Try it your way to give a meal that extra kick.

3 Tbsp	45 mL	vegetable oil
1 tsp	5 mL	black onion seeds
1	large onion, finely sliced into rings
8	red chilies, seeded and chopped
2 Tbsp	30 mL	finely chopped ginger
5	large tomatoes, finely chopped
1 tsp	5 mL	sugar
1 tsp	5 mL	sea salt
1 tsp	5 mL	dry urad daal, coarsely ground (use a mortar and pestle)

TEMPERING

2 Tbsp	30 mL	sesame oil
1 tsp	5 mL	black mustard seeds
1 tsp	5 mL	roasted sesame seeds
2	sprigs curry leaves, chopped

1. Heat the vegetable oil in a large, deep skillet (or karahi) over medium-high heat.

2. Add the black onion seeds and onion and sauté for 3–6 minutes.

3. Add the chilies and ginger and sauté for another 4 minutes.

4. When the onions are sautéed, add the chopped tomatoes and sauté for at least 10 minutes.

5. Add the sugar, salt and the urad daal, then set aside.

6. For the tempering, heat the sesame oil in a small saucepan on medium-high. When the oil is hot, add the mustard seeds, sesame seeds and curry leaves. Cook for about 30 seconds and then pour over the tomato mixture. Serve warm or cold. *Makes about 3 cups (750 mL)*

Mortar and pestle, used to coarsely grind daal

Nushi's Tangy Chutney

1. Place the sliced lemons in a large bowl and add the salt, lemon juice, turmeric and chilies, mixing well. Cover and set aside in a cool place (such as your basement, your pantry or even your garage) to marinate for 1 week.

2. In a bowl or container large enough to combine all the ingredients, add the celery, onions, green onions, cilantro, parsley, green and red peppers and garlic. Add the marinated sliced lemons. Stir to combine.

3. Add some of the mixture to a food processor or blender (you will have to work in batches). Add some of the vinegar with each batch to help with the processing. Note: Do not add water; the lemon juice and vinegar provide the right consistency and also act as a preservative.

4. Place the lemon mixture in a large bowl and add the crushed tomatoes. Add salt and chilies to taste.

5. Fill sterilized jars and store in the refrigerator. It keeps for a very long time thanks to the vinegar and lemon juice. *Makes about 8 cups (2 L)*

This simple and delicious relish-like pickle has a very lemony flavor. This is a specialty of my cousin Nushi, and this chutney accompanies most of the meals at her place. I particularly enjoy it with kebabs. Remember to make this ahead of time since it needs to marinate for one week.

4	large lemons, cut into thin slices
1 tsp | 5 mL	sea salt
2 cups | 500 mL	fresh lemon juice
2 tsp | 10 mL	turmeric
3 Tbsp | 45 mL	coarsely crushed dried red chilies
8	stalks celery, chopped
2	large onions, chopped
1 bunch	green onions, chopped
1 bunch	cilantro, chopped
1 bunch	parsley, chopped
1	green bell pepper, chopped
1	red bell pepper, chopped
10	cloves garlic
2 cups | 500 mL	white vinegar
1	28 oz (796 mL) can chopped tomatoes

Mango Pickles

❉ *Keri Ka Achaar*

20–30	green mangoes
2½ cups | 625 mL	salt
12	medium carrots
1	medium green papaya

MASALA

8 cups | 2 L	vegetable oil
¼ cup | 60 mL	garam masala (see page 173)
1 cup | 250 mL	coriander seeds, coarsely ground
½ cup | 125 mL	black mustard seeds, coarsely ground
¾ cup | 185 mL	salt
1½ cups | 375 mL	garlic paste (see page 177)
2 cups | 500 mL	red chili powder
3 Tbsp | 45 mL	black peppercorns
2½ Tbsp | 37 mL	fenugreek seeds
½ cup | 125 mL	turmeric powder

Memories come rushing back whenever I make this pickle. As children, we would eat some of the raw mango pieces, dipping them in salt, before my mother would start the pickling process. The taste of freshly made mango pickles with a meal of daal and rice was simply divine. This pickle will keep for months—even up to one year—in a cool, dry place in your pantry. This pickle takes three days to prepare, but do this once and it will last you a whole year! A few hours of work can give you a year-round supply of delicious mango pickle with enough to spare for guests. This is something to make in the summer since you have to dry the mangoes in the sun.

1. Wash the mangoes thoroughly and dry them. Cut each mango into quarters and remove the pit. Cut each piece in half again, giving a total of 8 pieces for each mango.

2. Put the mango pieces in a large plastic bucket or other nonreactive container and sprinkle with 1 cup (250 mL) of the salt, making sure the mangoes are well coated.

3. Wash and peel the carrots. Cut each carrot into 3 strips lengthwise and then cut each strip into at least 5 pieces. Put them in a separate nonreactive container and sprinkle with 1 cup (250 mL) of the salt, making sure the carrots are well coated.

4. Peel the green papaya. Cut it in half and remove all the seeds. Cut the papaya into strips just like the carrots. Place in a separate nonreactive container with the remaining ½ cup (125 mL) of salt, making sure the papaya is well coated with the salt.

5. Set all the containers aside for 1 day in a cool place.

6. The next day, remove the mango, carrot and papaya pieces and spread them on a plastic sheet to dry out in the sun for 1 day.

7. When the mango, carrot and papaya pieces have dried out nicely, make the masala.

8. Heat the oil over medium-high heat in a stock pot large enough to accommodate all the dried fruit and vegetables. When the oil is really hot, add all the masala ingredients: the garam masala, coriander seeds, black mustard seeds, salt, garlic paste, red chili powder, peppercorns, fenugreek seeds and turmeric powder. Cook and stir the masala for at least 5 minutes, then turn off the heat and allow the oil to cool to room temperature.

9. When the masala has cooled, add the mangoes, carrots and papaya. Mix well to coat them with the masala.

10. Pour the pickles into large sterilized canning jars. Fill at least three-quarters of the jar with the mango and carrots, then make sure the mixture is completely covered by a layer of masala oil. This should come up to 1 inch (2.5 cm) above the mangoes. If there is not enough oil, heat more vegetable oil until it is really hot, let it cool completely and then use it to cover the pickles. This way the pickles will keep for up to 1 year—but I am pretty sure they will be gone within 6 months. *Makes enough for about 8–10 large canning jars*

Pickled Mangoes & Carrots

✳ Sambaro

You may think of pickles as pickled cucumbers, but in India, pickling all kinds of fruits and vegetables is extremely common. Serve these spicy pickles with any rice dish; they are so delicious they can also be eaten on their own or with a naan or roti. If you wish to make them milder, reduce the green chilies to 4 or 5. These pickles will keep in the refrigerator for at least a week, but believe me, they will be finished before that.

2	green mangoes
4	medium carrots
2	celery stalks
2	Granny Smith apples
½ head	small cabbage
10	green chilies
1 tsp	5 mL	salt
1 tsp	5 mL	turmeric
½ cup	125 mL	vegetable oil
1 tsp	5 mL	black mustard seeds
½ tsp	2 mL	fenugreek seeds
12	curry leaves
6	dried red chilies
1 tsp	5 mL	cumin seeds
1½ tsp	7 mL	garlic paste (see page 177)
½ tsp	2 mL	sugar

1. Wash the mangoes and pat them dry. Cut them in half and remove the pit in the middle. Cut mango into strips about 3 inches (7.5 cm) long and ½ inch (1 cm) wide. Set aside in a large dish.

2. Prepare the carrots, celery and apples the same way as the mangoes and add them to the dish.

3. Shred the cabbage and add to the mixture.

4. Wash the green chilies, pat them dry and cut them in half lengthwise. Do not deseed them. Set aside in a separate bowl.

5. Add the salt and turmeric to the fruit and vegetable mixture. Mix well, then add the green chilies and mix well. (Avoid getting chilies on your hands by using a spoon or wearing gloves.)

6. Heat the oil in a large, deep skillet (or karahi) over medium-high and add the black mustard seeds and fenugreek seeds.

7. When the seeds begin to pop, immediately add the curry leaves, dried chilies, cumin seeds and garlic paste. Sauté for about 30 seconds.

8. Add the vegetables and cook, partially covered, for at least 15 minutes or until the mangoes become limp.

9. Sprinkle with the sugar and sauté for about 10–15 minutes or until the moisture has evaporated. Transfer to a glass dish or jar. Chill and serve cold. *Makes about 8 cups (2 L)*

Quick Mango Pickles

❋ Aam Achaar

Green mango is delicious either raw or cooked. In this popular Gujarati-style condiment, the rock-hard green type of mango is used. You could try this with yellow-fleshed mangoes if you prefer a sweeter taste.

1	large green mango
½ tsp	2 mL	salt
½ tsp	2 mL	red chili powder

1. Peel and slice the mango into long thin slivers.

2. Sprinkle with salt and red chili powder.

3. Serve as an accompaniment to any meal. *Makes about 1 cup (250 mL)*

Raita

Raita is a great accompaniment to many Indian dishes. Its main ingredient is yogurt and can help cool an overspiced palate if you choose to leave out the chilies. Raita goes very well with rice, tandoori and vegetable dishes, as well as with many appetizers, such as samosas and pakoras.

2 cups	500 mL	plain yogurt
1	small cucumber, finely diced
2–3	green chilies, finely diced (optional)
1	small onion, finely diced
2 sprigs	cilantro, finely chopped
2 sprigs	mint, finely chopped
½ tsp	2 mL	salt
½ tsp	2 mL	ground black pepper
1 tsp	5 mL	sugar
2 Tbsp	30 mL	fresh lemon juice
½ tsp	2 mL	chaat masala (see page 175)

1. In a large bowl, combine the yogurt, cucumber, green chilies (if using), onion, cilantro, mint, salt, pepper, sugar, lemon juice and chaat masala.

2. Chill before serving. *Makes about 2 cups (500 mL)*

Garam Masala 173

Curry Masala Paste 174

Chaat Masala 175

Rasam Powder 175

Tandoori Powder 176

Ginger Paste 176

Garlic Paste 177

Onion Purée 177

Seasonings, Spices & Pastes

In this section, I've included recipes for fresh spice mixtures. These recipes are for people who plan to do a lot of Indian cooking and want to have fresh spice mixtures on hand. When you prepare these mixtures ahead of time, you'll save a lot of time later on.

In India we grind our spices by crushing them with a smaller round or cylindrical stone on a very large, flat, heavy stone in the shape of a tray. The grinding stone can be replaced by a coffee grinder for dry spices or with a blender for wet pastes.

Garam Masala

1. Put all of the spices into a small skillet and dry-roast over very low heat for about 1 minute. Let cool for 5 minutes.

2. Grind to a fine powder in a coffee grinder. Store in an airtight jar at room temperature. This will keep for about a year, but I would recommend using it up before that since ground spices gradually lose their aroma.
   Makes about 1 cup (250 mL)

TAHERA'S TIPS
Grinding spices with a mortar and pestle might be authentic, but it's also very time-consuming and labor intensive. I have a coffee grinder that I use only for grinding spices and I highly recommend it. Otherwise your coffee may never taste the same again.

Garam masala is a combination of different aromatic spices ground together. You can buy it anywhere, but it will never be the same as making your own. Make sure to use good quality spices.

½ cup | 125 mL	green cardamom pods
2 Tbsp | 30 mL	black peppercorns
1 Tbsp | 15 mL	whole cloves
3	cinnamon sticks (3 inches/8 cm)
¼ cup | 60 mL	fennel seeds
2	nutmeg nuts

Curry Masala Paste

½ cup ǀ 125 mL	coriander seeds
½ cup ǀ 125 mL	white cumin seeds
1 cup ǀ 250 mL	vegetable oil
¼ cup ǀ 60 mL	turmeric
3 Tbsp ǀ 45 mL	garlic powder
1 Tbsp ǀ 15 mL	ginger powder
1 Tbsp ǀ 15 mL	ground black pepper
1 Tbsp ǀ 15 mL	paprika
1 Tbsp ǀ 15 mL	garam masala (see page 173)
1 Tbsp ǀ 15 mL	sugar
1 tsp ǀ 5 mL	salt
1 cup ǀ 250 mL	vinegar
½ cup ǀ 125 mL	water

1. Dry-roast the coriander and cumin seeds in a skillet over medium-high heat.

2. Let the seeds cool and then grind them in a coffee grinder.

3. Heat ½ cup (125 mL) of the oil in a saucepan until hot, but not smoking.

4. Add the coriander and cumin powder, turmeric, the garlic and ginger powders, ground black pepper, paprika, garam masala, sugar and salt. Sauté for about 30 seconds. Reduce the heat and add the vinegar and water. Cook, stirring occasionally, for at least 6–7 minutes, or until the liquid is reduced and the oil floats on top.

5. Cool the mixture to room temperature before pouring the paste into small, sterilized glass jars.

6. Heat the remaining ½ cup (125 mL) of oil and pour enough into each jar to cover the paste. Store in the freezer and use as required. *Makes 4 cups (1 L)*

Chaat Masala

2 Tbsp | 30 mL	cumin seeds
2 Tbsp | 30 mL	salt
½ tsp | 2 mL	asafetida (see page 22)
2 tsp | 10 mL	red chili powder
¼ cup | 60 mL	dried mango powder
2 tsp | 10 mL	dried mint
1 Tbsp | 15 mL	ground ginger

1. Dry-roast the cumin seeds in a frying pan on medium-high for about 1 minute until almost golden brown.

2. Mix with the remaining ingredients and grind them into a fine powder using a mortar and pestle or a coffee grinder. Store in a glass container. *Makes ⅔ cup (160 mL)*

Rasam Powder

This mixture makes a cook's daily preparation of the different varieties of rasam easy (see page 38 for one of my recipes). I prepare the rasam masala powder in bulk and store it in a glass container for everyday use.

1 cup | 250 mL	dried chilies
½ cup | 125 mL	roasted cumin seeds
½ cup | 125 mL	roasted dry urad daal
1 Tbsp | 15 mL	black peppercorns
½ cup | 125 mL	black mustard seeds
2 Tbsp | 30 mL	roasted coriander seeds

1. Blend all the ingredients to a fine powder in a coffee grinder. Store in a glass container in a cool place for up to 6–8 months. *Makes about 1¾ cups (425 mL)*

Tandoori Powder

This hot blend of fragrant spices is used for Butter Chicken (page 57) and tandoori fish, chicken or prawns.

2 tsp | 10 mL	turmeric
1½ tsp | 7 mL	garam masala (see page 173)
½ tsp | 2 mL	Spanish saffron
½ tsp | 2 mL	paprika
¾ tsp | 4 mL	red chili powder
¾ tsp | 4 mL	ground cardamom
¾ tsp | 4 mL	garlic powder

1. Combine all the spices and store in an airtight jar in a cool, dry place. *Makes about 2 Tbsp (30 mL)*

TAHERA'S TIPS
Not all saffron is the same. Be sure to use Spanish saffron in this recipe. It's the really good stuff and it's worth its weight in gold.

Ginger Paste

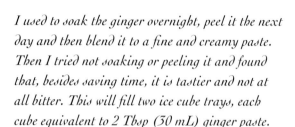

I used to soak the ginger overnight, peel it the next day and then blend it to a fine and creamy paste. Then I tried not soaking or peeling it and found that, besides saving time, it is tastier and not at all bitter. This will fill two ice cube trays, each cube equivalent to 2 Tbsp (30 mL) ginger paste.

2 lb | 1 kg	ginger (if possible, use ginger with pink skin)
1½ tsp | 7 mL	salt
1 cup | 250 mL	water

1. Clean the ginger, but do not peel it. Cut it into small chunks (to make it easy to blend).

2. Put the ginger into a food processor or blender, add the salt and water and blend until a smooth paste forms.

3. Spoon the mixture into ice cube trays and freeze.

4. When the cubes are firm, remove them and store in resealable plastic bags in the freezer until required. *Makes 2 cups (500 mL)*

Garlic Paste

The flavor of this garlic paste is just as good as fresh garlic. It's easy to prepare in advance and can be frozen in an ice cube tray—a convenient size for later use. This recipe will fill four ice cube trays and each cube is equivalent to about 2 Tbsp (30 mL) of garlic paste, or 2 cloves of garlic.

3 lb | 1.5 kg	garlic
¾ cup | 185 mL	white vinegar

1. Peel the garlic and purée the cloves in a blender or food processor while gradually adding the vinegar.

2. Spoon the mixture into ice cube trays and freeze.

3. When the cubes are firm, remove them and store in resealable plastic bags in the freezer until required. *Makes 4 cups (1 L)*

Onion Purée

Onion purée is used to achieve a creamy texture in many Kashmiri and Lahori curries. I like to make large amounts and freeze it in large ice cube trays. This recipe yields enough to fill four ice cube trays and each cube is the equivalent of 2 Tbsp (30 mL).

12	medium onions
1 cup | 250 mL	water

1. Peel the onions and cut into chunks. Combine the onions and water in a large saucepan over high heat and bring to a boil. Boil for 5 minutes. Stir occasionally.

2. Drain the onions and allow to cool. Transfer to a blender or food processor and purée for 2–3 minutes, until creamy. Process in batches if necessary.

3. Spoon the mixture into ice cube trays and freeze.

4. When the cubes are firm, remove them and store in resealable plastic bags in the freezer until required. *Makes 4 cups (1 L)*

Almond & Honey Pastries (*Kataifi*) 180

Date Balls 181

Mawa Pastry 182

Caramel Custard & Milk Pudding 185

Rose Milk Custard (*Basindi*) 187

Floating Island Pudding (*Fulfaludo*) 188

Sweet Rice Pudding (*Kheer*) 191

Custard Pie 192

Sweet & Creamy Semolina Dessert (*Sooji Halwa*) 194

Crème de la Crème (*Rabri*) 195

Shahi Tukray 196

No-Bake Sweet Milk Fudge (*Penda*) 198

Pistachio Barfi (*Pista Barfi*) 200

Almond Halwa (*Badam Halwa*) 201

Habshee Halwa 202

Milk Cake (*Kalakand*) 203

Semolina Cake 204

Indian Profiteroles in Saffron Syrup (*Kalimati*) 205

Golden Milk Balls in Syrup (*Gulab Jamun*) 206

Cocktail Fruit Juice 207

Milk Cloud 208

Pistachio & Almond Milk (*Pista Badam*) 210

Mango Lassi 211

Black Cardamom Coffee (*Qahawah*) 211

Sweets, Desserts & Drinks

Almond & Honey Pastries

❄ Kataifi

This is a dessert to die for—it's absolutely delicious. Every happy occasion in Indian life revolves around sweets, be it an announcement of a birth, a marriage or any other good news. Make this dessert part of your own special occasion.

2 cups | 500 mL	ground almonds
½ tsp | 2 mL	ground cardamom
½ cup | 125 mL	paneer, crumbled (see page 17)
¼ cup | 60 mL	sugar
1	egg white
1	16 oz (45 g) package kataifi pastry, thawed
¼ lb | 250 g	unsalted melted butter
1½ cups | 375 mL	honey

1. Combine the ground almonds, cardamom, paneer and sugar in a bowl. In a separate bowl, beat the egg white lightly and add it to the almond mixture, combining well. Divide the mixture into 4 portions.

2. Remove the pastry from its package. Shake it loose to make it fluffy. Divide it into 4 portions. Cover with a damp cloth to keep it from drying out.

3. Preheat the oven to 350°F (180°C). Grease a baking sheet.

4. Form one portion of the pastry into a rectangle, about 12 × 8 inches (30 × 20 cm). Place one portion of the almond mixture along the long edge of the rectangle.

5. Gently roll it up, making sure to twist it as you roll it so that the mixture stays inside. Place the roll on the baking sheet. Repeat with the remaining portions. Cut each portion into 3 or 4 pieces.

6. Brush the pastry with melted butter and bake for about 40 minutes, or until golden brown.

7. Meanwhile, warm the honey in a small saucepan over medium heat. Remove from the oven and spoon warm honey over the top of each pastry. Cover the pastries with foil until cool. *Make 12–16 pastries*

TAHERA'S TIPS

Kataifi pastry is shredded phyllo dough that looks a bit like vermicelli. You can find it in Greek or Middle Eastern specialty stores. Believe me: don't try to make it yourself.

Date Balls

1. Melt the butter in a large saucepan over medium heat. Add the dates, sugar and salt. Cook, stirring constantly, until the mixture forms a smooth paste, about 5 minutes.

2. Remove the pan from the heat and add the Rice Krispies, vanilla and nuts. Stir to combine.

3. Allow the mixture to cool slightly, then form small balls. Roll each date ball in coconut and cool. *Makes about 50 date balls*

VARIATION

You can use any one kind of nuts you like—try cashews, pecans, almonds, pistachios or walnuts. Or you can use a combination of them, which is what I prefer. Instead of rolling date balls just in coconut, try using ground pistachios or almonds or all three. For a festive look, make the balls small enough to fit in to tiny foil or paper cups.

This is a sweet that is usually made during the month of Ramadhan when it is customary to break a fast by popping a date into your mouth. This rich and tasty morsel is just the perfect snack-sized dessert for entertaining and serving over the holidays.

1 cup	250 mL	butter
1 lb	500 g	dates, pitted and chopped
¾ cup	185 mL	sugar
pinch	salt
2 cups	500 mL	Rice Krispies cereal
1 tsp	5 mL	vanilla
1½ cups	375 mL	chopped mixed nuts
¾ cup	185 mL	unsweetened desiccated coconut

Mawa Pastry

This rich Gujarati dessert is very popular in East Africa during the Diwali festival and the Idd celebration. I have introduced it to many of my friends, who have responded with rave reviews. Here's hoping you like it too.

PASTRIES

2½ Tbsp	37 mL	semolina (Cream of Wheat)
1½ Tbsp	22 mL	ground almonds
2 cups	500 mL	whole milk
2 Tbsp	30 mL	sugar
½ cup	125 mL	rose water
½ tsp	2 mL	saffron threads
1		16 oz (450 g) package puff pastry

SYRUP

½ cup	125 mL	sugar
¾ cup	185 mL	water
¼ tsp	1 mL	ground cardamom

GARNISH

½ cup	125 mL	slivered almonds

FOR THE PASTRIES

1. In a medium-sized saucepan over medium heat, combine the semolina, ground almonds and milk. Bring to a boil.

2. Simmer, stirring occasionally, until the mixture starts to thicken and become creamy, about 4–5 minutes. Add the sugar, rose water and saffron and continue to cook for another 5 minutes.

3. Preheat the oven to 375°F (190°C). Grease a baking sheet.

4. Roll out the puff pastry thinly, about ¼ inch (6 mm) thick, and cut into circles with a cookie cutter or glass (about 4 inches/10 cm in diameter). Place 1 tsp (5 mL) of the cream of wheat mixture on each circle. Fold the bottom edge over the top and pinch to seal.

5. Place the pastries on the baking sheet and bake for 25–30 minutes until golden brown.

FOR THE SYRUP

1. While the pastries are baking, prepare the syrup by bringing the sugar and water to a boil in a saucepan over medium heat.

2. Let boil for about 6 minutes, stirring continuously. Stir in the ground cardamom, remove from the heat and set aside to cool.

TO FINISH THE PASTRIES

1. Remove the pastries from the oven and brush or drizzle with the syrup. Sprinkle with the slivered almonds. Return to the oven for 10 minutes.

2. Remove and cool on a wire rack. *Makes 16 small pastries*

Caramel Custard & Milk Pudding

1. Combine the 3 cups (750 mL) of whole milk and the evaporated milk in a large saucepan over high heat. Bring to a boil.

2. When the milk is at a full boil, reduce the heat to medium and continue cooking until the milk is reduced to about three-quarters of the original amount, about 45 minutes. Add the sugar and vanilla and stir until the sugar is dessolved.

3. Whisk together the custard powder and the ¼ cup (60 mL) whole milk in a small bowl, making sure to whisk out any lumps. Add the custard mixture to the boiling milk and cook for 1 minute, whisking continuously.

4. Stir in the cardamom and remove from the heat; set aside for about 30 minutes.

5. Preheat the oven to 350°F (180°C).

6. Combine the ¾ cup (185 mL) sugar and ¼ cup (60 mL) water in a small, heavy saucepan over medium heat. Cook for approximately 10 minutes, or until the syrup thickens and turns amber in color, stirring occasionally.

7. While the syrup is cooking, place an 8-inch round deep cake pan in the oven to warm. When the syrup is ready, immediately pour it into the warmed dish, turning the dish in all directions to coat the bottom and sides with the caramel.

(continued on next page)

I learned to make this delicious pudding from my mum, and since then it's been a family favorite during the fasting month of Ramadhan. Try it with fresh seasonal berries and make a memorable ending to your festive dinner.

3 cups | 750 mL	whole milk
1	13 oz (370 mL) can evaporated milk
½ cup | 125 mL	sugar
½ tsp | 2 mL	vanilla paste (see page 186)
1 tsp | 5 mL	pure vanilla extract
2 tsp | 10 mL	custard powder
¼ cup | 60 mL	whole milk
½ tsp | 2 mL	ground cardamom
¾ cup | 185 mL	sugar
¼ cup | 60 mL	water
5	large eggs
	seasonal berries (optional)

8. Whisk the eggs in a large dish until nice and frothy. Add to the slightly cooled custard and stir well. Be sure to complete this step after coating the casserole dish with the caramel, so that it has cooled before adding the custard; otherwise the eggs will start to cook when they are added to the dish.

9. Pour the custard into the caramel-coated dish, place it in the oven and bake for 40 minutes.

10. Cool to room temperature and then chill in the refrigerator for at least 3–4 hours. Turn the custard out onto a serving dish. Serve with berries of your choice, if desired. *Serves 8*

Rose Milk Custard

✳ Basindi

1. Combine the cream, condensed milk, whole milk and custard powder in a large saucepan over medium heat. Use a whisk to mix it well and bring it to a smooth consistency while simmering.

2. Add the yellow food coloring, ground cardamom and rose essence. Continue to simmer, stirring constantly, about 10–15 minutes. The mixture should be thick and coat the back of a spoon. If it is too thin, whisk ¼ cup (60 mL) of water with 1 tsp (5 mL) of custard powder in a separate bowl, and gradually add it to the boiling mixture, stirring continuously until it thickens.

3. Remove the custard from the heat and pour it into a serving dish (with or without fruit) and then sprinkle the mixed almonds and pistachios over it. Chill for a few hours before serving. *Serves 8*

TAHERA'S TIPS
Only found in Indian stores, rose essence is stronger than rose water; you only use a few drops, otherwise it is overpowering.

This northern Indian recipe was very popular during the time of the maharajahs in Rajasthan. In East Africa we also prepare this dessert during the fasting month of Ramadhan, and serve it later in the evening after breaking our fast. In India it is usually served over fresh fruit, whereas in East Africa it's either served on its own, over faludo (a vegetarian gelatin) or over pieces of fruit-flavored Jell-O.

4 cups | 1 L	half-and-half cream
1	10¼ oz (300 mL) can sweetened condensed milk
1 cup | 250 mL	whole milk
1 tsp | 5 mL	custard powder
¼ tsp | 1 mL	yellow food coloring (optional)
¼ tsp | 1 mL	ground cardamom
1–2 drops	rose essence
to serve	fresh fruit (try kiwi, strawberries or melon) cut into bite-sized pieces (optional)
½ cup | 125 mL	slivered almonds or pistachios (or a combination)

Floating Island Pudding

Fulfaludo

Meringues, creamy custard, candied fruits and nuts, all drizzled with caramel—this recipe has it all and is a perfect dessert for that special occasion.

VANILLA CUSTARD

3½ cups | 875 mL	whole milk
¾ cup | 185 mL	granulated sugar
1 tsp | 10 mL	vanilla extract
½ tsp | 2 mL	ground cardamom
1½ Tbsp | 22 mL	custard powder
12	egg yolks (reserve the egg whites)

FLOATING ISLAND MERINGUES

16 cups | 4 L	water
12	(reserved) egg whites
1¾ cups | 425 mL	granulated sugar
pinch	sea salt

(ingredients continued on page 190)

FOR THE VANILLA CUSTARD

1. In a large saucepan, whisk together the milk, sugar, vanilla and ground cardamom. Add the custard powder and whisk thoroughly to remove any lumps. Bring to a boil over medium-high heat, stirring continuously.

2. In a separate large saucepan, thoroughly beat the egg yolks. Gradually add the boiling milk mixture to the beaten egg yolks and stir constantly over low heat.

3. Continue stirring over low heat until the custard thickens, about 10 minutes. Remove from the heat and continue stirring for at least 5 minutes to avoid lumps. Set aside.

FOR THE MERINGUES

1. Bring the water to a boil in a large saucepan over medium-high heat.

2. Using an electric mixer, beat the egg whites in a large bowl until soft peaks form.

3. Add the sugar and salt gradually, continuing to beat until the peaks are stiff and glossy.

4. Using two tablespoons or a small mold, shape the meringues and drop them in the boiling water. Cook for 2 minutes, then flip and cook for another 2 minutes. Remove and place on paper towels to drain.

(continued on page 190)

TO FINISH THE DISH (OPTIONAL)

2 Tbsp	30 mL	slivered pistachios
2 Tbsp	30 mL	chopped red and green maraschino cherries
2 Tbsp	30 mL	slivered almonds
2 cups	500 mL	granulated sugar
6 Tbsp	90 mL	water

TAHERA'S TIPS

You can grind the pistachios in a coffee grinder to make this even easier. A little patience is required to put this dessert together, but it will be rewarded with a impressive, decadent dish.

TO FINISH THE DISH (OPTIONAL)

1. Pour the custard in a large casserole or glass dish and sprinkle the chopped pistachios over the custard. Gently arrange the meringues on the custard. Decorate with the cherries and slivered almonds.

2. Combine the sugar and water in a small saucepan and bring to a boil, stirring continuously until it becomes thickened and golden in color; this could take up to 10 minutes. When a thick caramel forms, reduce the heat remove from heat and drizzle over the meringues. Chill before serving. *Serves 7–8*

Sweet Rice Pudding

❋ *Kheer*

1. Rinse the rice and run your fingers through it to loosen the grains.

2. Combine the rice and the half-and-half cream in a large saucepan and bring to a boil over medium-high heat, stirring constantly so it doesn't stick. Reduce the heat to low and continue cooking for about 30 minutes.

3. Remove the rice from the heat and beat with an electric mixer. Add the sugar, nutmeg, cardamom, saffron and about 1 Tbsp (15 mL) of the almonds.

4. Add the whipping cream and simmer for a few minutes over low heat.

5. Pour the rice pudding into a glass bowl or casserole dish and decorate it with pistachios and the remaining almonds. Serve warm. *Serves 6–8*

This is a very rich dish that is served on festive occasions. Serve it with Puri (page 147).

½ cup | 125 mL	basmati rice, soaked overnight
4 cups | 1 L	half-and-half cream
1¼ cups | 310 mL	sugar
¼ tsp | 1 mL	ground nutmeg
¼ tsp | 1 mL	ground cardamom
pinch	crushed saffron threads
¼ cup | 60 mL	finely chopped almonds
4 cups | 1 L	whipping cream (35%)
¼ cup | 60 mL	finely chopped pistachios

Custard Pie

This dessert is without a doubt one of the best-known sweet dishes from the Middle East. Remember, don't waste your money and buy expensive packaged semolina. It can be found cheaply in the bulk section.

3 cups | 750 mL	whole milk
½ cup | 125 mL	caster (superfine) sugar
¾ cup | 185 mL	semolina (Cream of Wheat)
½	cinnamon stick (2 inches/5 cm)
2 Tbsp | 30 mL	unsalted butter
1 Tbsp | 15 mL	lemon zest
1 Tbsp | 15 mL	vanilla extract
5	medium eggs
14 sheets	phyllo pastry
1 cup | 250 mL	unsalted butter, melted

SYRUP

¾ cup | 185 mL	caster sugar
½ cup | 125 mL	water
1 tsp | 5 mL	fresh lemon juice
2–3 drops	yellow food coloring (optional)

1. Combine the milk, sugar, semolina and cinnamon stick in a large saucepan over medium heat. Bring to a gentle boil, stirring constantly and cook for about 3 minutes.

2. Add the 2 Tbsp (30 mL) butter and the lemon zest and vanilla. Cook, stirring constantly, for 3–4 minutes longer.

3. Remove from the heat, remove the cinnamon stick, cover and let cool to room temperature, about 30 minutes.

4. Whisk the eggs in a bowl and stir into the cooled custard mixture.

5. Preheat the oven to 375°F (190°C) and grease an ovenproof 9- × 13-inch (3.5 L) casserole dish.

6. Place a phyllo sheet in the dish and brush with melted butter. Continue layering phyllo, brushing each with butter, until you have 7 sheets in the dish.

7. Pour the custard mixture over the sheets and layer the remaining 7 sheets of pastry on top, brushing each with melted butter.

8. Using a pizza cutter or small knife, mark the top with either diamond or square shapes. Make sure you do not cut too deep into the pastry.

9. Spray lightly with water and bake for 25–30 minutes or until the top is golden brown. Remove and cool to room temperature.

10. To prepare the syrup, bring the sugar and water to a boil in a medium saucepan over medium-high heat, stirring occasionally. When the mixture starts to boil, add the lemon juice and food coloring and continue boiling for about 12–15 minutes, or until a thick syrup forms. The syrup should almost coat the back of the spoon, but it should not be caramelized. Cool the syrup at room temperature for about 15 minutes before pouring over the custard. Refrigerate and serve cold. *Serves 6–8*

Sweet & Creamy Semolina Dessert

❋ Sooji Halwa

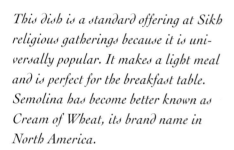

This dish is a standard offering at Sikh religious gatherings because it is universally popular. It makes a light meal and is perfect for the breakfast table. Semolina has become better known as Cream of Wheat, its brand name in North America.

¼ cup | 60 mL	ghee or unsalted butter
1 cup | 250 mL	semolina (Cream of Wheat)
¾ cup | 185 mL	water
3 Tbsp | 45 mL	raisins
1 Tbsp | 15 mL	unsweetened desiccated coconut
2 Tbsp | 30 mL	slivered almonds
½ tsp | 2 mL	ground cardamom
½ cup | 125 mL	sugar

1. Combine the ghee and semolina in a saucepan over medium heat. Stir continuously until it turns light brown in color, about 10 minutes.

2. Add the water, raisins and coconut and cook for another 10 minutes, stirring continuously, until all of the water is fully absorbed and the semolina grains swell.

3. Add 1 Tbsp (15 mL) of the almonds and the cardamom and sugar and continue stirring until the sugar is dissolved and the ingredients are well combined.

4. Remove from the heat, pour into serving dishes and garnish with the remaining almonds. Serve hot. *Serves 6*

VARIATION

There are several variations of Sooji Halwa. To make a richer version, try adding 1 cup (250 mL) of grated carrots and substitute whole milk for the water. Add a little more sugar and ½ tsp (2 mL) of nutmeg and you have yourself a rich, sweet dessert.

Crème de la Crème

* Rabri

1. Bring the cream and milk to a boil in a large, deep skillet (or karahi), stirring continuously. Bruise the cardamom pods by lightly pressing them with the side of a knife and add them to the saucepan.

2. Boil and stir for another 10–15 minutes, then reduce the heat to medium or medium-low.

3. Use a wooden spoon to pull the skin off the surface of the mixture and to the side. Continue cooking and removing the skin until the liquid is reduced by about half; this will take about 60 minutes. Stir in the sugar and continue cooking and stirring for another 5 minutes to ensure the sugar melts quickly and does not stick to the bottom and burn (it will smell burnt if this happens and spoil the taste).

4. Add the kewra essence and half of the almonds and pistachios. Stir and boil for 2 minutes.

5. Pour into a large serving dish and decorate the top with the remaining chopped nuts and pistachios. Cool to room temperature, then refrigerate for a few hours or overnight before serving. *Serves 4–6*

TAHERA'S TIPS
When you have to heat milk in a saucepan, rinse the pan with water first to prevent the milk from sticking.

Out of India's best-known desserts, this one is my favorite. I like it just plain and chilled, but you can add tropical fruit of your choice before serving. I recommend serving it with sitafor (custard apple) or chopped mango. You will need a nonstick wok or karahi to achieve the best results. Note: I always make Rabri the day before I will be serving it. Not only does it allow it to thicken, but the flavor of the kewra essence is always better the next day. (Don't leave out the kewra!)

1 cup | 250 mL	half-and-half cream
6 cups | 1.5 L	whole milk
2	green cardamom pods
7 Tbsp | 105 mL	sugar
2 Tbsp | 30 mL	kewra essence (see page 210)
½ cup | 125 mL	chopped, blanched almonds
½ cup | 125 mL	chopped pistachio nuts

Shahi Tukray

This is no doubt India's most exotic dessert. Shahi Tukray is very well known with the Nawabis (moguls and rich ruler of ancient India). This dessert is loaded with nuts, raisins and khoya and can be served hot or cold. Sometimes it is decorated with edible silver. Make this treat a part of your own special occasion.

1 loaf	sliced white bread
1 cup | 250 mL	vegetable oil
8 cups | 2 L	whole milk
1½ cups | 375 mL	sugar
½ cup | 125 mL	finely chopped pistachios
½ cup | 125 mL	slivered almonds
½ cup | 125 mL	raisins
½ tsp | 2 mL	saffron threads
½ tsp | 2 mL	ground cardamom
1½ cups | 375 mL	grated khoya (see below)
2–3 sheets	varakh (optional; see page 203)

1. Remove all the crusts from the bread and cut the slices in half diagonally to create triangles.

2. Heat the oil in a large skillet over medium-high heat and fry the triangles until golden brown. Drain on paper towels.

3. In a large saucepan, bring the milk to a boil, then reduce the heat to low and cook until it reduces by about one-quarter, about 6 cups (1.5 L).

4. Add the sugar and return to a boil.

5. Combine the pistachios, almonds and raisins in a bowl and add about half of this mixture to the milk. Add the saffron and ground cardamom. Mix well and remove from the heat.

6. Lay the fried bread in 9- × 13-inch (3.5 L) casserole dish and sprinkle half the grated khoya over it. Gently pour the milk overtop of the khoya layer, making sure not to break the pieces of bread. Sprinkle the remaining khoya and nut-raisin mixture on top. Finally, decorate with varakh (edible silver foil) if desired. Chill for at least 2 hours before serving. *Serves 6–8*

TAHERA'S TIPS

Khoya (also called mawa) is solid dried milk, which is grated before use. It is the base for many kinds of decadent Indian sweets. You can find it in the frozen food section of Indian grocery stores.

No-Bake Sweet Milk Fudge

* Penda

I have made this fudge for a lot of parties. It's easy and quick to make and, as a bonus, when made with the skim milk powder, it has fewer calories!

¼ cup | 60 mL	butter (preferably unsalted)
¼ cup | 60 mL	cream cheese
1 tsp | 5 mL	vanilla extract
½ cup | 125 mL	granulated sugar
¼ cup | 60 mL	unsweetened desiccated coconut
1½ cups | 375 mL	skim milk powder
to decorate	ground pistachios, ground nutmeg, silver balls, or pecans (optional)

1. Beat together the butter, cream cheese, vanilla and sugar in a large glass bowl until smooth, creamy and light.

2. Add the coconut and milk powder to form a doughy mixture. You want it to be thick enough to handle.

3. Form into about 20 balls, slightly flatten the top and place in small paper cups. Decorate, if desired, by sprinkling with a little nutmeg, ground pistachios, silver balls or pecans.

4. Refrigerate in a plastic container for up to 1 week. *Makes about 20 pieces*

Habshee Halwa
(page 202)

Pistachio Barfi
(page 200)

No-Bake Sweet Milk Fudge
(facing page)

Pistachio Barfi

* Pista Barfi

This is a delicious and rich Indian sweet that is often made with cashews, mango or coconut. If you like, you can use a mixture of almonds and pistachios.

1 cup	250 mL	butter
1 tsp	5 mL	ground cardamom
1		15 oz (475 g) carton ricotta cheese (whole milk ricotta is best)
1½ cups	375 mL	sugar
4 cups	1 L	milk powder
1 cup	250 mL	pistachios, crushed
1 drop		green food coloring (optional)
2½ Tbsp	37 mL	milk

1. Melt the butter in a saucepan over low heat and add the cardamom. Add the ricotta cheese and stir until the cheese melts. Add the sugar while continuing to stir. Then slowly start adding the milk powder, stirring constantly. When all the ingredients are well combined, add the pistachios. Dissolve the green food coloring in the milk and add to the saucepan.

2. Continue cooking over low heat until the mixture thickens. Do not overcook or the barfi will become too hard when set. The mixture should be soft and glossy.

3. Spread the mixture into a greased 9- × 13-inch (3.5 L) casserole dish and cool. Cover with plastic wrap when cool.

4. Let sit at room temperature for a day, then cut into small squares. *Makes 24 squares*

Almond Halwa

❊ Badam Halwa

1. Mix the cornstarch, sugar, water and lemon juice in a large saucepan and bring to a boil over medium-high heat, stirring constantly to avoid the mixture from forming lumps. Cook and stir continuously for 5 minutes, then reduce the heat to medium.

2. Add the slivered almonds, cardamom, cardamom seeds, saffron, oil and food coloring (if using). Stir vigorously so the mixture does not stick to the pan.

3. Continue cooking and stirring for about 25 minutes. By this time it will be a thick, sticky mass that is virtually lifting out of the pan. Remove from the heat.

4. Lightly grease a 9- × 13-inch (3.5 L) casserole dish. Use two large wooden spoons to lift the halwa from the saucepan and into the casserole dish. Decorate the top with the whole blanched almonds.

5. Allow to cool slightly before serving. To serve, moisten a spoon with warm water and spoon into bowls. *Serves 8*

TAHERA'S TIPS
You can refrigerate the leftovers. To serve, simply warm on high for 1 minute in the microwave.

Halwa means "sweet" and is used to describe various kinds of Indian confections. This is one of the most exotic Indian halwas, with a taste that cannot be matched. Eaten hot or cold, it is a gourmet's delight.

2 cups | 250 mL	cornstarch
3 cups | 750 mL	sugar
8 cups | 2 L	water
2 tsp | 10 mL	fresh lemon juice
1 cup | 250 mL	slivered almonds
1½ tsp | 7 mL	ground cardamom
4	cardamom pods, opened and seeds removed
½ tsp | 2 mL	saffron threads
¾ cup | 185 mL	vegetable oil
1 tsp | 5 mL	yellow food coloring (optional)
1 cup | 250 mL	whole blanched almonds

Habshee Halwa

Finally I have managed to get this wonderful recipe, which no chef has been willing to part with. A big thank you to Zarina Alloo for sharing it. It is easy, tasty and a dessert to die for. Note that the total cooking time could be up to one hour.

1½ cups	375 mL	butter
6		eggs, beaten
3 cups	750 mL	sugar (must be exact)
3 cups	750 mL	milk powder (use good quality)
1½ cups	375 mL	slivered almonds (or another nut of your choice)
½ tsp	2 mL	ground cardamom
¼ tsp	1 mL	ground nutmeg
½ tsp	5 mL	saffron threads (or to taste)
¼ cup	60 mL	slivered almonds (optional)
¼ cup	60 mL	chopped pistachios (optional)

1. Preheat the oven to 300°F (150°C).

2. Melt the butter in a large ovenproof dish (such as a Dutch oven) over medium-high heat. Turn off the heat, add the eggs and mix well. Add the sugar, milk powder, the 1½ cups (375 mL) of almonds, cardamom, nutmeg and saffron. Stir well to combine.

3. Place the dish in the preheated oven for 20 minutes.

4. Remove the dish, stir the mixture and return to the oven. Continue to cook for another 35–40 minutes, stirring the mixture every 10–15 minutes.

5. When done the mixture should be brown and leave the sides of the pot, forming a ball. Also, the butter will begin to separate from the mixture.

6. Spread the mixture on a large baking sheet, smooth it out and allow to cool.

7. Cut into squares or diamond shapes and serve it in a decorative dish. If you like, sprinkle some chopped or sliced almonds and pistachios over the top. *Serves 6–8*

Milk Cake

1. Bring the cream and milk to a boil in a large saucepan over medium-high heat. When it has been at a full boil for about 4 minutes, add the fruit salt. Heat for another 30 minutes, stirring constantly, until reduced to about 2½ cups (625 mL).

2. Let the mixture cool for about 30 minutes, then add the brown sugar, half the butter (2 Tbsp/30 mL), maple syrup, cardamom and milk powder. Mix until smooth. Return to the stove over medium heat for 10 minutes, stirring constantly to prevent it from sticking.

3. When the mixture becomes thick and draws away from the sides of the pan, remove from the heat. Add the remaining 2 Tbsp (30 mL) of butter and mix well.

4. Pour into a greased cake pan or mold; cover with a tea towel and let set for 3–4 hours at room temperature.

5. To remove the cake from the mold, immerse the pan in boiling water for 30 seconds and then ease the cake onto a glass plate. Decorate with chopped pistachios and almonds, and with varakh (edible silver foil) if desired.

Makes 1 medium cake, about 16 pieces

TAHERA'S TIPS

Varakh (edible silver foil) is for decorative purposes only and, if you want to spend the money, it's impressive. Apply it by handling the attached wax sheet (otherwise it will stick to your fingers). Gently place the foil on the food; then peel off the wax paper. Varakh can be found at Indian grocery stores, usually at the counter near the cashier. If you're a vegetarian, make sure to use varakh that is manufactured without using animal products.

According to the halwais (sweets-makers) I talked to, this dish hails from Uttar Pradesh, which is on the Nepalese–Indian border. There are a lot of different versions of this beautiful cake. Mine is not only fairly quick, but delicious too. Enjoy it.

1 cup | 250 mL	half-and-half cream
4 cups | 1 L	whole milk
¼ tsp | 1 mL	Eno fruit salt (see page 21)
1 cup | 250 mL	brown sugar
¼ cup | 60 mL	salted butter
¼ cup | 60 mL	maple syrup
1½ tsp | 7 mL	freshly ground cardamom
4 cups | 1 L	skim milk powder
½ cup | 125 mL	mixed chopped pistachios and almonds
1 sheet	varakh (optional)

Semolina Cake

I used to enjoy this cake at almost every birthday party with my Greek friends when I was living in Zaire.

3 Tbsp	45 mL	water
¼ cup	60 mL	orange juice
1 Tbsp	15 mL	orange zest
¾ cup	185 mL	butter
¾ cup	185 mL	caster (superfine) sugar
4		eggs
1¾ cups	425 mL	semolina (Cream of Wheat)
¾ cup	185 mL	all-purpose flour
3½ tsp	17 mL	baking powder
½ cup	125 mL	milk
3 Tbsp	45 mL	slivered (or chopped) almonds
¼ cup	60 mL	halved, blanched almonds, for decoration

SYRUP

2½ cups	625 mL	sugar
2½ cups	625 mL	water
2 Tbsp	30 mL	fresh orange or lemon juice

1. Preheat the oven to 350°F (180°C). Grease a 7- × 11-inch (18 × 28 cm) cake pan.

2. Combine the water with the orange juice and zest.

3. Using an electric mixer, cream together the butter, sugar, orange juice and zest until light, fluffy and creamy.

4. Beat in the eggs, one at a time; this should take approximately 7–10 minutes.

5. Fold in the semolina, flour and baking powder. Fold in the milk and the slivered almonds.

6. Spread the mixture evenly in the greased cake pan.

7. Arrange the halved almonds on the top and bake for about 40–45 minutes, until the cake is golden and shrinks from the sides of the pan. Remove from the oven and cool on a rack.

8. To make the syrup, bring the sugar, water and orange or lemon juice to a boil in a medium-sized saucepan over medium-high heat. Boil until the syrup has thickened slightly, about 25 minutes. Set aside to cool.

9. Prick the cake in several places with a skewer and pour the syrup over the cake. Cut into squares or diamond shapes and serve cold. *Serves 6–8*

VARIATION

You can also flavor the syrup with rose water if you like. It's simply a matter of taste. If you want to use rose water, use about ½ cup (125 mL).

Indian Profiteroles in Saffron Syrup

* *Kalimati*

1. To make the profiteroles, mix the flour and yeast together in a mixing bowl and gradually add enough of the 1 cup (250 mL) of water to form a thick smooth batter.

2. Cover and set aside in a warm spot to rise until the batter is about double in size, about 1½ hours.

3. Meanwhile, prepare the syrup by combining the sugar, the ¾ cup (185 mL) of water, cardamom, saffron and food coloring in a saucepan over medium-high heat. Bring to a boil and cook until the mixture forms a fairly thick and sticky syrup, about 15–20 minutes. Stir constantly while cooking. Set aside to cool slightly.

4. Heat the oil in a large, deep skillet (or karahi) over medium-high heat.

5. Using a tablespoon (or your hand moistened with water), form small balls of the batter and drop them in the oil. Deep-fry until golden brown all over and about double in size.

6. Drain well on paper towels and then dip them in the syrup. Serve hot. *Serves 10*

Very quick and easy to prepare, kalimati is both impressive and decadent. The charm of this dessert is that when you bite into one of these profiteroles, you have to continually wipe your chin to stop the syrup from rolling down!

1½ cups | 375 mL	all-purpose flour
1 tsp | 5 mL	instant yeast
1 cup | 250 mL	water (approximately)
1 cup | 250 mL	sugar
¾ cup | 185 mL	water
½ tsp | 2 mL	ground cardamom
¼ tsp | 1 mL	saffron threads
2–3 drops	yellow food coloring (optional)
4 cups | 1 L	oil for deep-frying

Golden Milk Balls in Syrup

❈ *Gulab Jamun*

This delicately scented dessert is very popular all over the world and was first introduced in royal kitchens. The saffron and almonds—both prized ingredients—signify that this is a dish meant for special occasions. The dessert is fried and then soaked in a sweet syrup.

1½ cups | 375 mL	powdered milk
½ cup | 125 mL	all-purpose flour
1 tsp | 5 mL	baking powder
pinch	ground cardamom
pinch	ground nutmeg
1 cup | 250 mL	whipping cream (35%)
2 cups | 500 mL	vegetable oil (for deep-frying)

SYRUP

1½ cups | 375 mL	water
1½ cups | 375 mL	sugar
2–3 drops	yellow food coloring (optional)
2–3 drops	rose essence (see page 187)
2–3	saffron threads
¼ cup | 60 mL	slivered almonds

1. Combine the powdered milk, flour, baking powder, cardamom and nutmeg in a bowl.

2. Add the whipping cream little by little until a soft dough is formed. You may not need to use all of the whipping cream.

3. Moisten your palms with the remaining whipping cream to keep the dough from sticking to your hands. Knead the dough well in the bowl and form into small balls (about the size of a walnut).

4. Heat the oil in a large, deep skillet (or karahi) over medium heat. Deep-fry the balls until they are golden brown, about 30–40 seconds.

5. To make the syrup, combine the water, sugar, a few drops of the yellow food coloring, a few drops of the rose essence and a few threads of saffron in a saucepan. Bring to a boil and continue to stir the syrup over high heat for about 15 minutes, until thickened. Let the syrup cool slightly.

6. Arrange the balls on a platter and drizzle the syrup overtop. Garnish with slivered almonds. *Serves 6*

Cocktail Fruit Juice

1. Blend all the ingredients except the ice until smooth in a blender or food processor.

2. Divide the ice among tall glasses, pour in the juice and serve with straws. *Serves 6*

TAHERA'S TIPS
You can buy orange blossom water at Indian food stores and at some supermarkets.

A jug of chilled cocktail fruit juice is often served at the end of a grand meal like those served during Idd or Diwali, or at weddings or other special functions. This drink is great for special occasions, but it also hits the spot in the heat of summer.

4	ripe bananas, peeled
2 cups | 500 mL	pineapple juice
1 small	papaya, peeled, seeded and chopped
1 cup | 250 mL	passion fruit juice
5–6	strawberries
2 cups | 500 mL	orange juice
¼ cup | 60 mL	sugar
pinch	salt
½ cup | 125 mL	orange blossom water
4 cups | 1 L	crushed ice

Milk Cloud

This is a popular beverage in Lahore, where it is usually served at weddings. I use an electric beater to make it frothy, but in India and Pakistan the chefs pour the milk from one pot to another. An expert can span 2 to 3 feet (60 to 75 cm) without spilling a drop!

6 cups | 1.5 L	whole milk
⅔ tsp | 2 mL	ground cardamom
2 drops	pink food coloring
⅔ cup | 160 mL	sweetened condensed milk
¼ tsp | 1 mL	rose essence (see page 187)
1	6 oz jar (170 g) clotted cream (optional)
1 Tbsp | 15 mL	finely chopped almonds
1 Tbsp | 15 mL	finely chopped pistachios

1. Bring the milk to a boil in a large saucepan over medium-high heat, stirring continuously. Boil for about 20 minutes, until it's reduced almost by half.

2. Stir in the ground cardamom and food coloring, mixing well. Stir in the condensed milk. Stir in the rose essence and remove from the heat. Cool to room temperature.

3. When cool, mix in the clotted cream, if using, and refrigerate for a few hours.

4. Before serving, beat with an electric beater till frothy, approximately 7–10 minutes.

5. Pour into goblets and sprinkle with the chopped nuts. Serve immediately. *Serves 4*

TAHERA'S TIPS

Clotted cream, also called Devonshire or Devon cream, is available at most grocery stores.

Pistachio & Almond Milk

❋ *Pista Badam*

This refreshing milk usually is served during a festive season or at weddings. This beverage is delicious whether served warm or icy cold.

8 cups | 2 L	whole milk
1	14 oz (398 mL) can evaporated milk
½ cup | 125 mL	sugar
½ tsp | 2 mL	freshly ground cardamom
½ tsp | 2 mL	saffron threads
2–3 drops	kewra essence (see below)
½ cup | 125 mL	coarsely ground pistachios
½ cup | 125 mL	crushed almonds
½ tsp | 2 mL	vanilla extract
2–3 drops	pink food coloring (optional)
4 cups | 1 L	crushed ice (if serving cold)

1. Bring the whole milk and evaporated milk to a boil in a large nonstick saucepan over medium-high heat. Boil for at least 20 minutes, stirring often to ensure it does not burn on the bottom.

2. Add the sugar and ground cardamom and boil for a further 10–12 minutes. Pour half of the milk into another saucepan.

3. Add the saffron and kewra essence to one saucepan. Allow to sit, stirring occasionally, until a sweet aroma arises from it and the color is a rich pale yellow.

4. Add half of the pistachios and crushed almonds. Mix well and pour into fancy teacups and serve warm.

5. Cool the other half of the boiled milk and pour into a jug. Add the vanilla extract and the remaining pistachios and almonds to the jug. Stir in the pink food coloring until it becomes a pale pink color. Mix well and chill in the refrigerator for 2–3 hours.

6. To serve, fill serving glasses half full with crushed ice, pour the milk over it and provide large straws to ensure the nuts get through. *Serves 6*

TAHERA'S TIPS

Kewra is also known as kevda essence and is an aromatic extract made from pandanus flowers. Just like rose water, it is often added to desserts and beverages in Indian and Southeast Asian cuisine. You can find it at Indian grocery stores.

Mango Lassi

There is no substitute—not here, and not even in India—for this popular drink. It's very refreshing either on its own or served with hot, spicy foods. Be sure to make this when mangoes are in season.

3 cups	750 mL	plain yogurt
¼ cup	60 mL	sugar
2½ cups	625 mL	mango pulp
¾ tsp	4 mL	ground cardamom
1½ cups	375 mL	crushed ice
3 cups	750 mL	cold water

1. Combine the yogurt, sugar and mango pulp in a large bowl and whisk vigorously with a large whisk until the mixture is smooth (or combine in a food processor).

2. Add the ground cardamom, crushed ice and water and continue to whisk for 2 minutes.

3. Add the water and stir well. Refrigerate and serve chilled. *Serves 6*

Black Cardamom Coffee
❊ *Qahawah*

This strong-tasting beverage, prepared mostly with Arabica coffee, is the drink that's usually served to guests on the island of Zanzibar. This recipe is one of the most traditional ways of preparing it.

2 cups	500 mL	water
1 Tbsp	15 mL	finely ground roasted coffee
½ tsp	2 mL	ground cardamom
1 tsp	5 mL	sugar

1. Put all the ingredients in a saucepan and bring to a boil over medium heat. Boil for at least 10 minutes.

2. Serve hot in small traditional coffee cups, or in any small cup. *Serves 2*

Index

Afghanistani Sweet Bread, 154

African Donuts (*Mandazi*), 150–152

ajowan seeds, 2, 14

Almond & Honey Pastries (*Kataifi*), 180

Almond & Vegetable Curry (*Sabji Badam Kadhi*), 119

Almond Halwa (*Badam Halwa*), 201

Arabic-Style Samosas (*Sambosay Arabi*), 26–28

asafetida, 22

Baked Beef Kebabs (*Dum Ke Kebabs*), 72

Barbecued Chicken on Skewers (*Reshmi Kebabs*), 58

basmati rice, 84–85. *See also* rice dishes

beans, 7

    Crispy Lentil-Stuffed Pastries, 23–24

    guvar beans, 4, 106

    Lentil & Flat Bean Curry, 106

    Rajastani Daal, 103

    Red Kidney Bean Curry, 108

    Royal Curry, 109

    Sudanese-Style Fava Beans, 104

beef

    Baked Beef Kebabs, 72

    Bihari Beef Kebabs, 73

    in Chicken Vindaloo, 50

    Tender Beef Skewers, 66

beef, ground

    Arabic-Style Samosas, 26–28

    Crispy Meatballs, 77

    Galawati Kebab, 70

    Lacey Kebabs, 69

    Lucknowi-Style Rice, 89

    Macaroni Meat Pie, 74–76

    Mogul Hamburgers, 67

    Royal Kedgeree, 96–97

    Sausage Rolls, 31–32

Bengali Bread (*Luchis*), 153

Bihari Beef Kebabs, 73

Black Cardamom Coffee (*Qahawah*), 211

Bombay Nuts 'n' Bolts (*Chevdo*), 12–13

Bombay Potatoes (*Alu Mumbai Masala*), 123

breads, 142

    gluten-free, 155–159

    quick breads, 144–148

    sweet, 154, 205, 206

    wheat-free, 155–159

    yeast breads, 143, 149–152, 154

bulghur wheat, 46

butter, 7, 8

Butter Chicken (*Makhani Murg*), 57

Buttermilk Curry (*Gujarati Kadhi*), 125

cakes and squares

    Almond Halwa, 201

    Habshee Halwa, 202

    Milk Cake, 203

    No-Bake Sweet Milk Fudge, 198

    Pistachio Barfi, 200

    Semolina Cake, 204

Caramel Custard & Milk Pudding, 185–186

carrots

    Mango Pickles, 166–167

    Pickled Mangoes & Carrots, 168

Casserole-Style Prawn Pilau, 98

Cauliflower & Pea Curry (*Matar Gobi Masala*), 113

Cauliflower with Potatoes (*Alu Gobi Masala*), 111

Chaat Masala, 175

chana daal, 4. *See also* lentils

    Bombay Nuts 'n' Bolts, 12–13

    Coconut Dosas, 158–159

chana flour, 18

cheese

    Almond & Honey Pastries, 180

    Cheese Bread, 149

    Macaroni Meat Pie, 74–76

    Paneer Butter Masala, 126

    Paneer Poppers, 15

    Spicy Indian Cheese, 17

Cheese Bread, 149

chicken, 7

    Barbecued Chicken on Skewers, 58

    Butter Chicken, 57

    Chicken in Green Curry, 52

    Chicken Karahi, 56

Chicken Vindaloo, 50
Dhansak Daal, 60–61
Half-Moon Chicken Pastries, 33–34
in Tender Beef Skewers, 66
Pakistani-Style Rice, 90–92
Spiced Saffron Rice with Chicken, 93–95
chicken, ground
Coconut Dosas, 158–159
Curried Chicken Kebabs, 51
Moroccan Chicken Pie, 54–55
Chicken in Green Curry (*Hare Masale Ki Murg*), 52
Chicken Karahi, 56
Chicken Vindaloo (*Murg Vindaloo*), 50
chilies, green, 51
chilies, Kashmiri, 3, 61
chutneys, 63, 162–165
citric acid crystals, 13
clarified butter, 8
Cocktail Fruit Juice, 207
coconut
Coconut Dosas, 158–159
Fresh Green Chutney, 162
Red Coconut Chutney, 163
Spiced Bean & Cucumber Salad, 41
Spiced Cucumber Salad with Mango, 42
Coconut Dosas, 158–159
coconut milk, 8
Green Peas in Coconut Curry, 117
Pigeon Peas in Coconut Sauce, 110
coffee, 211
cooking methods, tempering, 80
cream. *See* custards and puddings

Crème de la Crème (*Rabri*), 195
Crispy Lentil-Stuffed Pastries (*Gujarati Kachori*), 23–24
Crispy Meatballs (*Kali Kebabs*), 77
Crispy Savory Tidbits (*Nimki*), 14
cucumber
Spiced Bean & Cucumber Salad, 41
Spiced Cucumber Salad with Mango, 42
Spicy White Radish & Cucumber Salad, 44
Curried Chicken Kebabs (*Tikka Murg Kebabs*), 51
curries, 8
chicken, 51–52
lamb, 81
vegetarian, 102–119, 122, 125
Curry Masala Paste, 174
Custard Pie, 192–193
custards and puddings
Caramel Custard & Milk Pudding, 185–186
Crème de la Crème, 195
Custard Pie, 192–193
Floating Island Pudding, 188–190
Rose Milk Custard, 187
Shahi Tukray, 196
Sweet & Creamy Semolina Dessert, 194
Sweet Rice Pudding, 191

daal. *See* lentils; chana daal
Date & Tamarind Chutney (*Khajur Imli Chatni*), 162
Date Balls, 181
desserts. *See* cakes and squares; custards and puddings; pastries
Dhansak Daal, 60–61
dosas, 156–159

drinks, 207–211
drumsticks, 4, 132
Drumsticks in Sambaar (*Singhu Sambaar*), 130–132
Drumsticks with Potatoes (*Alu Singhu Masala*), 133

egg dishes
Potato & Egg Curry, 112
eggplant
Dhansak Daal, 60–61
Drumsticks in Sambaar, 130–132
Masala Eggplant, 136
Spiced Roasted Eggplant, 135
Spicy Eggplant with Yogurt, 137
Stuffed Eggplant Hyderabadi-Style, 138
Eno fruit salt, 21

fava beans, 104
fenugreek, 2, 118
fish. *See also* seafood
Kerala-Style Baked Salmon in Green Chutney, 63
flaky pastry, 31–32
Floating Island Pudding (*Fulfaludo*), 188–190
Fresh Green Chutney (*Lila Chatni*), 162
fruit drinks
Cocktail Fruit Juice, 207
Mango Lassi, 211

Galawati Kebab, 70
Garam Masala, 173
Garlic Paste, 177
ghee (clarified butter), 8
Ginger Paste, 176
gluten-free breads, 155–159

Golden Milk Balls in Syrup (*Gulab Jamun*), 206
Green Peas in Coconut Curry (*Naryal Matar Kadhi*), 117
guvar beans, 4, 106

Habshee Halwa, 202
Half-Moon Chicken Pastries, 33–34
hamburgers, 67

Indian Profiteroles in Saffron Syrup (*Kalimati*), 205
ingredients, Indian pantry, 2–5

Kashmiri Lamb Curry, 81
Kerala-Style Baked Salmon in Green Chutney, 63
kewra essence, 210
kidney beans
    Rajastani Daal, 103
    Red Kidney Bean Curry, 108
    Royal Curry, 109
kokam, 106

Lacey Kebabs (*Jhali Kebabs*), 69
lamb. *See also* mutton
    in Tender Beef Skewers, 66
    Kashmiri Lamb Curry, 81
    Lamb Korma, 80
    Lamb Palak, 78
lamb, ground
    Arabic-Style Samosas, 26–28
    Mogul Hamburgers, 67
Lamb Korma, 80
Lamb Palak, 78
Lebanese Salad, 43
Leek Soup with Baby Potatoes & Cilantro, 40
lemons
    Nushi's Tangy Chutney, 165

Lentil & Flat Bean Curry (*Bhendi Guvar Daal*), 106
lentils (daal), 4, 5
    Bombay Nuts 'n' Bolts, 12–13
    Coconut Dosas, 158–159
    Crispy Lentil-Stuffed Pastries, 23–24
    Dhansak Daal, 60–61
    Drumsticks in Sambaar, 130–132
    Lentil & Flat Bean Curry, 106
    Onion Bread, 155
    Onion Dosas, 157
    Peppery Tamarind Soup, 38
    Pigeon Peas in Coconut Sauce, 110
    Rajastani Daal, 103
    Spinach & Lentil Daal, 102
Lucknowi-Style Rice (*Khima Biryani*), 89

Macaroni Meat Pie, 74–76
Mango Chutney (*Aam Chatni*), 163
Mango Lassi, 211
Mango Pickles (*Keri Ka Achaar*), 166–167
mangoes
    Mango Chutney, 163
    Mango Lassi, 211
    Mango Pickles, 166–167
    Pickled Mangoes & Carrots, 168
    Quick Mango Pickles, 169
    Spiced Cucumber Salad with Mango, 42
margarine, 7, 8
masala (spice mixture), 61
Masala Eggplant (*Baigan Masala*), 136
masoor daal, 4. *See also* lentils
    Spinach & Lentil Daal, 102
Mawa Pastry, 182–183

measuring, butter and margarine, 7
menu planning, 9
meringue, 188
Milk Cake (*Kalakand*), 203
Milk Cloud, 208
milk drinks
    Milk Cloud, 208
    Pistachio & Almond Milk, 210
Millet Bread (*Dhebra*), 148
Mogul Hamburgers (*Chapli Kebabs*), 67
Moroccan Chicken Pie (*Basteeya*), 54–55
mung beans, 13
mung daal. *See also* lentils
    Lentil & Flat Bean Curry, 106
    Spiced Bean & Cucumber Salad, 41
mutton. *See also* lamb
    in Chicken Vindaloo, 50
    in Dhansak Daal, 60–61

Naan, 143
No-Bake Sweet Milk Fudge (*Penda*), 198
Nushi's Tangy Chutney, 165

okra, 4, 129
Onion Bread (*Pesarattu*), 155
Onion Dosas, 157
Onion Fritters (*Piaz Pakora*), 22
Onion Purée, 177
onions
    deep-frying, 57
    Onion Bread, 155
    Onion Dosas, 157
    Onion Fritters, 22
    Onion Purée, 177
    Onion Salad, 47
    Potato & Onion Fritters, 21

Onion Salad, 47

Pakistani-Style Rice (*Peshawari Biryani*), 90–92
Paneer Butter Masala (*Makhani Paneer*), 126
Paneer Poppers, 15
Paratha, 145
parsley
    Tabouli, 46
pasta
    Macaroni Meat Pie, 74–76
pastries
    African Donuts, 150–152
    Almond & Honey Pastries, 180
    Arabic-Style Samosas, 26–28
    Crispy Lentil-Stuffed Pastries, 23–24
    Date Balls, 181
    Golden Milk Balls in Syrup, 206
    Half-Moon Chicken Pastries, 33–34
    Indian Profiteroles in Saffron Syrup, 205
    Mawa Pastry, 182–183
    Sausage Rolls, 31–32
Pea & Fenugreek Curry (*Matar Methi Malai*), 118
peas, green
    Cauliflower & Pea Curry, 113
    Green Peas in Coconut Curry, 117
    Pea & Fenugreek Curry, 118
Peppery Tamarind Soup (*Rasam*), 38
phyllo pastry
    Custard Pie, 192–193
    Moroccan Chicken Pie, 54–55
Pickled Mangoes & Carrots (*Sambaro*), 168

pickles, 166–169
pigeon peas. *See* toor daal
Pigeon Peas in Coconut Sauce (*Barazi*), 110
Pistachio & Almond Milk (*Pista Badam*), 210
Pistachio Barfi (*Pista Barfi*), 200
Potato & Egg Curry (*Alu Baida Kadhi*), 112
Potato & Onion Fritters (*Alu Piaz Pakora*), 21
Potato Curry (*Alu Ki Bhaji*), 122
potatoes
    Bombay Potatoes, 123
    Cauliflower with Potatoes, 111
    Dhansak Daal, 60–61
    Drumsticks with Potatoes, 133
    Leek Soup with Baby Potatoes & Cilantro, 40
    Lucknowi-Style Rice, 89
    Paneer Poppers, 15
    Potato & Egg Curry, 112
    Potato & Onion Fritters, 21
    Potato Curry, 122
    Stuffed Potato Kebab, 124
    Zanzibari Pilau, 99
prawns, 98
Puri, 147

Quick Mango Pickles (*Aam Achaar*), 169

radish, white (*mooli*), 4, 44
Raita, 169
Rajastani Daal, 103
Rajastani Spicy Okra (*Rajastani Bhindi Masala*), 129
Rasam Powder, 175
Red Coconut Chutney (*Laal Nariyal Chatni*), 163

Red Kidney Bean Curry (*Rajma Kadhi*), 108
rice, 7, 13, 84–85
rice dishes
    Casserole-Style Prawn Pilau, 98
    Coconut Dosas, 158–159
    Lucknowi-Style Rice, 89
    Onion Dosas, 157
    Pakistani-Style Rice, 90–92
    Rice with Fresh Lime, 86
    Royal Kedgeree, 96–97
    Spiced Saffron Rice with Chicken, 93–95
    Sweet Rice Pudding, 191
    Yogurt Rice, 88
    Zanzibari Pilau, 99
Rice with Fresh Lime (*Nimbu Chawal*), 86
rose essence, 187
Rose Milk Custard (*Basindi*), 187
Roti (*Chapati*), 144
Royal Curry (*Shahi Kadhi*), 109
Royal Kedgeree (*Moghlai Khichdi*), 96–97

saffron, 3, 176
salads
    Lebanese Salad, 43
    Onion Salad, 47
    Spiced Bean & Cucumber Salad, 41
    Spiced Cucumber Salad with Mango, 42
    Spicy White Radish & Cucumber Salad, 44
    Tabouli, 46
salmon, 63
samosas, 26–28
sauces
    chutneys, 63, 162–165

sauces *(continued)*
    white sauce, 33–34, 74–76
Sausage Rolls, 31–32
seafood
    Casserole-Style Prawn Pilau, 98
    Kerala-Style Baked Salmon in
        Green Chutney, 63
seasoning
    spice mixtures, 61, 172–177
    tempering, 80
semolina
    Semolina Cake, 204
    Sweet & Creamy Semolina
        Dessert, 194
Semolina Cake, 204
Shahi Tukray, 196
soups
    Leek Soup with Baby Potatoes &
        Cilantro, 40
    Peppery Tamarind Soup, 38
Spiced Bean & Cucumber Salad
    (*Kosumbri*), 41
Spiced Cucumber Salad with Mango
    (*Modern Kosumbri*), 42
Spiced Roasted Eggplant (*Baigan
    Bhartha*), 135
Spiced Saffron Rice with Chicken
    (*Moghlai Murg Biryani*), 93–95
Spiced Vegetable Medley (*Sabzi
    Jalfrezi*), 128
spice mixtures, 61, 172–177
Spicy Eggplant with Yogurt (*Dahi
    Baigan*), 137
Spicy Indian Cheese (*Paneer
    Tikka*), 17
Spicy White Radish & Cucumber
    Salad, 44

spinach
    Lamb Palak, 78

Spinach & Lentil Daal, 102
Spinach Fritters, 18
Spinach & Lentil Daal (*Palak Masoor
    Daal*), 102
Spinach Fritters (*Palak Pakora*), 18
Squash Kofta Curry (*Dudhi Kadhi
    Kofta*), 114–115
Stuffed Eggplant Hyderabadi-Style
    (*Rawayya*), 138
Stuffed Potato Kebab (*Alu
    Kofta*), 124
Sudanese-Style Fava Beans (*Foul
    Medammas*), 104
sugar syrup (*chasni*), 9
    Golden Milk Balls in Syrup, 206
    Indian Profiteroles in Saffron
        Syrup, 205
Sweet & Creamy Semolina Dessert
    (*Sooji Halwa*), 194
Sweet Rice Pudding (*Kheer*), 191

Tabouli, 46
tamarind, 3, 38
Tandoori Powder, 176
tempering, 80
Tender Beef Skewers (*Pursindah
    Sekhi Kebabs*), 66
Tomato Chutney (*Tamatar
    Chatni*), 164
tomatoes
    Peppery Tamarind Soup, 38
toor daal (pigeon peas).
    See also lentils
    Peppery Tamarind Soup, 38
    Pigeon Peas in Coconut
        Sauce, 110
turmeric, 3, 50

urad daal (white lentils), 5.
    See also lentils

Onion Bread, 155
Rajastani Daal, 103
use in dosas, 156

vanilla paste, 186
veal, 99
vegetable dishes
    Crispy Lentil-Stuffed
        Pastries, 23–24
    Leek Soup with Baby Potatoes &
        Cilantro, 40
    Royal Curry, 109
    Spiced Vegetable Medley, 128
vegetarian curries, 102–119, 122,
    125

wheat-free breads, 155–159
white sauce
    Half-Moon Chicken
        Pastries, 33–34
    Macaroni Meat Pie, 74–76

yeast breads, 143, 149–152, 154
yogurt
    Buttermilk Curry, 125
    cooking with, 8
    Mango Lassi, 211
    Raita, 169
    Spicy Indian Cheese, 17
    Yogurt Paratha, 146
    Yogurt Rice, 88
Yogurt Paratha (*Dahi Paratha*), 146
Yogurt Rice (*Dahi Chawal*), 88

Zanzibari Pilau, 99